MARK RAVENHILL

Shopping and Fucking

with commentary and notes by
DAN REBELLATO

B L O O M S B U R Y

LONDON · NEW DELHI · NEW YORK · SYDNEY

Bloomsbury Methuen Drama
An imprint of Bloomsbury Publishing Plc

50 Bedford Square	1385 Broadway
London	New York
WC1B 3DP	NY 10018
UK	USA

www.bloomsbury.com

This edition fi rst published in the United Kingdom in 2005 by Methuen Publishing Ltd
Reprinted by Bloomsbury Methuen Drama 2008, 2010, 2012, 2013

Shopping and Fucking first published in the United Kingdom in 1996 by Methuen

© 1996, 1997 by Mark Ravenhill
Commentary and Notes © 2005 by Dan Rebellato

British Library Cataloguing-in-Publication Data
A catalogue record for this book is available from the British Library.

ISBN: PB: 978-0-4137-7373-9
      ePDF: 978-1-4725-3660-0
      ePub: 978-1-4725-3659-4

Library of Congress Cataloging-in-Publication Data
A catalog record for this book is available from the Library of Congress.

Printed and bound in Great Britain

Contents

Dan Rebellato would like to thank Mark Ravenhill, Max Stafford-Clark, Philip Roberts, June Wright, and Aleks Sierz for their help in preparing this edition.

Mark Ravenhill: 1966–

1966   June: born in Haywards Heath, West Sussex.

1987   July: graduates from Bristol University, where he studied Drama and English.

      August: *Blood Brood*, short play (Edinburgh Fringe Festival: Carlton Centre).

1993   April: adapts *Mad Money* by Alexander Ostrovsky (BBC World Service).

      May: *Close to You*, short play (London New Play Festival: Old Red Lion).

1994   October: adapts *The Lulu Plays* (*Earth Spirit* and *Pandora's Box*) by Frank Wedekind (BBC World Service).

      December: *Fist*, short play ('I'll Show You Mine' Festival: Finborough Theatre).

1995   December: becomes Literary Manager of Paines Plough (until June 1997).

1996   May: directs *A Week with Tony* by David Eldridge (Finborough Theatre).

      September: *Shopping and Fucking* (Out of Joint: Royal Court Theatre Upstairs at the Ambassadors).

      October–November: *Shopping and Fucking* tours England.

1997   January: *Shopping and Fucking* returns to Royal Court Theatre Upstairs.

      April: *Faust* (Actors' Touring Company: Lyric Hammersmith Studio and national tour) [play later retitled *Faust is Dead*].

      June: *Shopping and Fucking* transfers to the West End, for a six-week run (Gielgud Theatre).

November: *A Desire to Kill on the Tip of the Tongue* (Ravenhill's translation of *Une envie de tuer sur le bout de la langue* by French playwright, Xavier Durringer) given a playreading at the Royal Court.

1998   January: *Shopping and Fucking* returns to the West End (Queen's Theatre).

February: second company takes the Out of Joint production of *Shopping and Fucking* on an international tour.

March: *Sleeping Around*, co-written with Hilary Fannin, Stephen Greenhorn, and Abi Morgan (Salisbury Playhouse and Donmar Warehouse, followed by national tour); David Blunkett, Education Secretary, criticises the British Council for giving financial support to the European tour of *Shopping and Fucking*.

September: *Handbag* (Actors' Touring Company: Lyric Hammersmith Studio and national tour).

1999   September: *Some Explicit Polaroids* (Out of Joint: New Ambassadors and national tour).

2000   May: *Lost and Found* (BBC2).

June: *North Greenwich*, short play (given as a play reading by Paines Plough in the 'Wild Lunch' series).

November: *Feed Me* (BBC Radio 3).

2001   August: *Mother Clap's Molly House* (National Theatre: Lyttelton).

December: presented *Oh Yes I Am!* (BBC Radio 4), documentary on the British pantomime.

2002   Summer: Becomes Artistic Associate at the National Theatre.

September: libretto for *Die Fledermaus* by Johann Strauss, directed by Calixto Bieito (Welsh National Opera: New Theatre, Cardiff).

2003   February: *Mother Clap's Molly House* transfers to the West End (Aldwych Theatre).

March: *Totally Over You* performed by several youth theatre groups – the first, Sir Frederic Osborn School, Welwyn Garden City – culminating in a youth theatre festival, 'Shell Connections', at the National Theatre in July (the Kildare Youth Theatre and South Wight Youth Theatre).

June: *The Cut*, short play (given as a play reading by Paines Plough in the 'Wild Lunch' series); directs Brecht's *The Mother* as part of the Royal Court's 'Playwrights' Playwrights' series of rehearsed readings.

2004   March: *Moscow*, short play (given one performance as part of the Royal Court International Playwrights' Season).

October: delivers the Shakespeare Lecture at the Cheltenham Festival of Literature under the title 'Paradise Forgotten', discussing the Edenic visions of *As You Like It* and *A Winter's Tale*.

Education, a monologue (given a reading as part of the 'National Headlines' season of topical verbatim monologues at the National Theatre).

2005   February: *Product*, short play (performed by the author as part of Paines Plough's 'Engage' season, also curated by Ravenhill, at the Menier Chocolate Factory, London).

March: *Citizenship* (performed by various school groups under the 'Shell Connections' scheme).

Plot

Scene One
Mark used to work in the City but is now a junkie; Lulu, his flatmate, and Robbie, his boyfriend, are trying unsuccessfully to feed him. They ask him to tell them the story of how he sees them in a supermarket and buys them from a fat man who calls them trash. He decides he's got to get off heroin and, although Lulu and Robbie feel rejected, leaves to get medical help.

Scene Two
Lulu is being interviewed for a job as a shopping-channel presenter by Brian, a man obsessed with the film *The Lion King*. He asks her to act and insists she takes some of her clothes off. The ready meals she has stolen fall out of her jacket but she persuades him she needs the job. He offers her a trial – he will give her something to sell and see how she does.

Scene Three
Robbie has been sacked from a burger chain because he provoked a customer, who attacked him. Lulu has the items Brian wants her to sell: 300 ecstasy tablets. Mark comes home while Robbie is counting the tablets for her. In trying to conquer his problems with addiction, Mark has come to believe that his desire for intimacy is one of those debilitating habits that he has to kick. It also appears that he was thrown out of the clinic for getting involved with another patient: he paid him so that he could lick his arse, a transaction which 'didn't mean anything'. Robbie is hurt by his rejection and takes two tablets. Lulu has

heated up two ready meals and tells Mark they can't be split so he goes off to get some food. Robbie assures Lulu there were 300 pills.

Scene Four
Mark is in Gary's bedsit. They made contact through a sex line, and have met for some 'live' action. Gary is a rent boy and Mark only wants sex without involvement. Gary offers Mark some cocaine, which Mark refuses. Although Mark doesn't have the going rate, he is allowed to lick Gary's arse. He discovers it's bleeding. Gary advises Mark to stay and wash his mouth out with champagne.

Scene Five
Lulu is late meeting Robbie in a pub. She comes in splashed with blood. She was in a 7-Eleven when a wino stabbed the woman behind the counter. She wishes she'd done something to help but she managed to steal some chocolate. Robbie offers to take the E to the club himself; she acquiesces gratefully, warning him not to take any himself.

Scene Six
Gary tells Mark that he was being abused by his stepdad. Mark doesn't want to hear because he doesn't want to become involved with him. He tries to explain and ends up comforting Gary.

Scene Seven
In Accident and Emergency, Lulu is tending to Robbie's wounds. Her initial assumption is that he was mugged but it soon transpires that in a rush of elated generosity (and having taken some of them himself) he gave away all the E and got beaten up when he'd run out. Lulu is furious.

Scene Eight
Gary explains how he tried to tell the social services that his stepdad

was raping him, and they offered him a leaflet. He ran away. He says Mark can sleep on the floor, they're friends, they can go shopping with the money he's won on the slot machines.

Scene Nine

Brian shows Lulu and Robbie a video of his son playing the cello and weeps at the beauty of it. He is clearly a dangerous man, he gives them a week to raise the money they owe him and leaves them to watch a video of someone who 'failed his test' being tortured.

Scene Ten

Robbie and Lulu have started a phone sex business. They are using all the world's stories – the Garden of Eden, *Romeo and Juliet*, the Tower of Babel – and they're making a lot of money.

Scene Eleven

Mark and Gary are in a changing room. Mark is trying on expensive clothes which Gary offers to buy him on stolen credit cards. Gary tells Mark he can kiss him. Mark realises it's love he feels for Gary and says he wants to develop a relationship based on mutual respect. But Gary doesn't want the same; he wants someone who'll look after him and fuck him so it hurts. He rejects Mark but Mark demands that Gary give him a blow job in the changing room. Gary reveals that he is fourteen.

Scene Twelve

The phones aren't ringing and Robbie finds out why: the mobiles are switched off and the landlines unplugged. They have nearly reached their target but Lulu wants a break. It turns out that one of her punters was masturbating to security-camera footage of the attack in the 7-Eleven. Robbie wants to turn the phones on; she tries to make him eat instead and pushes his face in the food. Mark and Gary

arrive. Robbie discovers that Mark isn't paying Gary. Gary says
Mark loves him. Robbie attacks Gary. Mark says he didn't say he
loved him and walks out. Gary says he wants someone stronger than
Mark. Robbie warns him that it could be an unobtainable dream but
offers to help him for a fee.

Scene Thirteen
Mark, Gary, Lulu and Robbie are playing Truth or Dare. Gary can't
describe what's in his head and breaks down in tears. Mark's story
about the most famous person he's fucked becomes an elaborate lie
about having sex with Fergie and (implicitly) Diana. Then Gary has a
second attempt, with the others putting his fantasy into words for
him: they describe seeing him dancing alone in a club, being bought
by a man and taken home blindfold, a version of the story from Scene
One. As the story starts to get rough Mark tries to rescue him,
offering gentle affection, but is rebuffed and takes cocaine from
Gary's pocket instead. They describe taking him home as their slave,
their possession. Robbie starts to fuck Gary. Then Mark takes over
until Gary demands to be fucked by his father and Mark violently
refuses to play that role. Gary reminds them that he's paying and
demands to be fucked with a knife or a screwdriver. Mark agrees to
it.

Scene Fourteen
Brian is pleased with them: they have repaid what they owe and, their
lesson having been learned – 'money is civilisation and civilisation
money' – he returns the cash to them. The three flatmates are left
alone and Mark tells a science fiction version of their story but this
time the slave is freed and cannot bear his freedom. There is no
mention of Gary. Robbie, Mark and Lulu feed each other their ready-
prepared meals for one.

Commentary

When *Shopping and Fucking* opened in the autumn of 1996, it placed Mark Ravenhill squarely at the heart of a new generation of British playwrights whose work had brought a distinctively contemporary tone to the stage, a new intensity and candour about sex and violence, and a darkly funny and fast-moving set of plays that glittered with the icons of popular culture. The group, which included writers like Sarah Kane, Joe Penhall, Patrick Marber, Nick Grosso, Rebecca Prichard and Anthony Nielson, was often commercially as well as critically successful, and had an impact internationally, their plays being performed across the world. Furthermore, *Shopping and Fucking* – helped by its wittily outrageous title – has insinuated itself into the popular consciousness more successfully than any play since John Osborne's *Look Back in Anger* in 1956, a play to which, in some respects, it bears a surprising resemblance.

Various labels have been applied to this group, some more successful than others: 'the drama of disenchantment', 'the theatre of urban ennui', 'the new brutalists', 'in-yer-face theatre', among others. All of them attempt to capture various aspects of the plays' sense of loss and negativity, as well as their assault on the audience's sensitivities and limits. But the variety of names also points to a central ambiguity in these plays: what are they trying to do? Are they purely trying to shock us? Are they documentary plays? Are they satires, teeming with moral purpose and righteous anger? Are they numbed by the collapse of political and moral certainty?

All of these questions, and more, may be asked of *Shopping and Fucking*, and they remind us that from the very start, underneath the praise, the critics seemed curiously confused about *Shopping and Fucking*. The reviews of the first production were, on the whole, extremely positive; no one doubted Ravenhill's ability to create strong dramatic situations, most people recognised the skill with which he juxtaposes moments of emotional horror with near-farcical comedy.

However, beneath this unity there was real disagreement about how the play actually worked. Some critics found the explicitness of the play part of its virtue; others thought it a distraction. Some found the play's structure solid and traditional; others found it trendily fragmented. Some saw an urgent and important moral message in the play; others described it as morally slight; still others thought it heavy-handed in the delivery of its message. The play's ambiguity is visible in a striking symptom of critics offering both negative and positive comments in the same breath: 'revolting but persuasive', wrote one; 'in its own hellish way, stirring and prophetic', added another.

It may seem surprising, at first glance, that *Shopping and Fucking* should seem so ambiguous. It does not have a complex or ambiguous narrative; the language is clear and accessible; the setting is contemporary and familiar. What continues to confuse some critics about this play is its *attitude* towards the events it describes. That the critics failed to understand a new play is hardly unprecedented, of course, but in this case it points us to what is distinctive about this play: a change of mode, a new kind of theatrical engagement with politics. The uncertainty evinced by the first set of critical reviews may be described as an inability to answer the question, is this a political play? Answering this question and understanding why Ravenhill had to write the play in this new style – and why it initially confused the critics – will help unlock some of the richness of *Shopping and Fucking*.

Political Theatre

A certain template for modern British political playwriting was set out in the 1970s. Socialist writers like David Hare, Howard Brenton, David Edgar and Trevor Griffiths wrote large-scale plays for some of the biggest stages in Britain. Although all of these writers began their work in subsidised theatres, they were also popular writers, many of their plays transferring to the West End and to television.

At the risk of submerging their very distinct authorial identities, it will be helpful to draw out some of the plays' shared features, because to do so will create a wider sense of the definitions of political theatre operating in the era before the *Shopping and Fucking* generation. It is a characteristic of many political plays of the 1970s that they are epic in scale: the action of the play covering several years, the cast of characters often very large. The twelve scenes that make up David Hare's *Plenty* (1978), for example, take us from occupied France in 1943 to a Blackpool hotel in 1962. Howard Brenton's *Weapons of Happiness* (1976) features twenty-eight characters, while *Epsom Downs* (1977) has well over forty. (Nowadays, in large part because of a sharp decline in arts funding since the 1970s, new plays are lucky to have more than five in the cast.)

But these large casts and these sprawling structures were not due to some pathological lack of economy. These writers held the socialist conviction that the present cannot be understood without reference to the past, because history has a shape and we do not forge our destinies alone. What these structures did was embody a vision of the world; the grand scale of these plays encouraged the audience to situate the individual characters within a large historical and social context. These plays very often featured large centrepiece confrontations between characters on major political issues but the debate was always supported by this epic structure that encouraged a recognition of historical movement, and a social structure in which these individual lives unfold.

Although we now live in an era which has almost forgotten the word 'socialism', it is important to understand that these playwrights were working in a decade which seemed to hold out a real possibility of fundamental socialist transformation. The growth of the counter-culture in the 1960s, protests against the Vietnam War, the rise of the feminist and anti-racist movements, and the increasingly polarised state of industrial relations in Britain encouraged many – on the right and the left – to think that British society was heading for its final decisive crisis. In short, many people believed we were on the verge of a revolution. Many of the most important plays of the decade – Brenton's *Magnificence* (1973) and *The Churchill Play* (1974), Hare's *Fanshen* (1975), or Griffiths's *Occupations* (1970) and *The Party* (1973), for example – were asking not 'Will there be a revolution?' they were asking 'What sort of revolution will it be?'.

Thatcherism and the consumer society

But then, as David Hare put it, 'history took a turn which nobody had predicted'. There was a revolution of sorts, but it was from the right rather than the left. The General Election of May 1979 swept the Conservatives to power under their leader, Margaret Thatcher. This government was by far the most right-wing government since the war and was determined to overturn the 'post-war consensus': this was a set of liberal-left beliefs that had been accepted by Labour and Conservative governments since 1945 and included a belief in the state ownership and support of industry, that the government should intervene to minimise unemployment, that the unions had as valid a voice as the employers, and that a civilised culture should take a permissive attitude to personal moral choice.

The Thatcher governments of the 1980s challenged this consensus at every turn. They initiated a major programme of privatisation, opening all sectors of the economy to commercial competition, breaking the power of the unions, preferring to let the market rather than the government decide prices, wages and levels of unemployment. This was a return to a Victorian kind of liberal economics (hence the label 'neo-liberalism') in which the market was the best judge of society's priorities. It marked a profound shift in the values of British culture and society as Thatcherites everywhere extolled the virtues of competition, individual choice, entrepreneurialism, and argued that the making of money was a moral duty.

Although these policies may sound narrowly economic, they brought about a subtle but pervasive shift in British culture. The post-war consensus held that the government had a role to intervene to protect its citizens against the worst effects of the free market. Justice, morality, freedom and equality were all values considered to require protection from rampant economic speculation.

The new ethos argued the opposite: that the market should be the final arbiter of all of our values and any attempt to 'buck the market' would only cause worse effects further down the line. Thus if people really wanted freedom, the market would provide it. If the market did not provide freedom, it could only be because people had not demanded it in their consumer choices.

Further, for a fully-functioning free market to operate, everything must be assigned an economic value, and the final result of this is to turn all values into economic values. Things that are hard to assign a monetary value to – say, art, love, faith or justice – are either changed into things that *can* be more easily bought and sold or they become increasingly marginal in a market society. Of course, if the proponents of the free market are right, this is nothing to be alarmed at. If the market is the only arbiter of real value, then by definition nothing of any real value can be lost in a market society.

The decline of the Left

It is certainly the case, however, that the consumerism of the 1980s played a part in dismantling the radical political culture of the 1970s. For one thing, the Conservatives believed that state arts funding was itself a misguided attempt to shield artists from the bracing winds of market reality. They reduced levels of funding and recommended seeking private donations and sponsorship to make up the shortfall. New plays, especially radically left-wing new plays, were hardly designed to attract business sponsorship, however, and the funding required to support the large-scale dramaturgy of these plays was no longer forthcoming. Plays dwindled in size and scale through the 1980s.

But, more subtly, there was a cultural shift which meant that the kind of plays that had won large audiences in the 1970s now seemed adrift from their audiences' sensibilities. There were many fine plays that used the epic style developed in the 1970s to anatomise the failure of the Left and the changes being wrought on British society; but ironically the very changes they were analysing were working to undermine the effectiveness of the theatrical style.

Those epic plays were structured to foster a sense of historical movement and collective power. But the consumer society that Britain was becoming was working in the opposite direction. Such a society constitutes its members as consumers whose most fundamental acts are acts of shopping. The American collage artist Barbara Kruger memorably captured this in a stark photographic montage she produced in 1987 which shows a hand holding up a small card bearing the deathless consumerist slogan, 'I shop therefore I am'. By reducing the individual to the far more narrow role of consumer, the market separates off and obscures both their allegiance to any group and their immersion in historical process. In the apparent absence of society and history, nothing matters to the consumer but the act of shopping.

While none of this disproved the analysis offered by the earlier generation of playwrights, it certainly made it harder for them to connect with an audience. Ravenhill has discussed the way in which audiences changed over the decade:

> The Royal Court plays of the Eighties were contributing to a debate, and everyone who saw them shared a political vocabulary. You can no longer assume that an audience will share that particular vocabulary – or *have* any political vocabulary, for that matter. There is a much more diverse understanding of what a play is and in some ways, that's good. In others, you lose something, because you don't get a sense that all those plays are talking to each other. They're quite scattered.
>
> (Quoted in Andrew Smith, 'Play for Today', *Observer Magazine*,
> 31 October 1999, p. 39)

By the end of the decade, the large-scale political play was firmly out of fashion; most theatre workers had drifted away from this form, often looking at far less content-based or obviously political theatre forms like performance art, physical theatre, or that exemplary theatrical form of the Thatcherite eighties, the megamusical.

At the beginning of the decade, as the neo-liberal experiment was getting under way, Thatcherites would steel one another's resolve with the code word 'TINA' – meaning: There Is No Alternative. The Left remained in disarray through much of the decade, the Labour Party irreconcilably split into rival factions, the non-parliamentary left fragmenting into special interest groups; it seemed that the Conservative mantra was increasingly apposite. In 1989, as the vast, vicious, corrupt and crumbling edifice of the so-called Communist bloc collapsed, it seemed that capitalism was unstoppable. The theatre critic Michael Coveney explained this fall from leftist certainty in stark terms: 'Hare and the rest knew in the Seventies what they were against. Now nobody knows. And nobody cares' (*Observer Review*, 9 February 1997, p. 13). The old Left promise of a good society, a better world, a kind of utopia was little more than a distant dream.

Searching for values

This world, in which money is all and individuals are just consumers, is the world of *Shopping and Fucking*. Ravenhill's characters spend a great deal of the play shopping and thinking about shopping (that is, of course, when they're not fucking) but other aspects of their identity seem much less sharply drawn. We know little or nothing about their own families, their jobs, their aspirations or beliefs, even their last names. They also seem to lack any sense of history, barely mentioning anything that isn't a feature of contemporary popular culture. It's as if history has been wiped from their minds.

There is one moment where the decline of the bigger picture is directly addressed, as Robbie tells Gary his view of the world:

> I think a long time ago there were big stories. Stories so big you could live your whole life in them. The Powerful Hands of the Gods and Fate. The Journey to Enlightenment. The March of Socialism. But they all died or the world grew up or grew senile or forgot them, so now we're all making up our own stories. Little stories. (p. 66)

As many critics have pointed out, this idea is taken very directly from one of the founding philosophical works of 'postmodernism', Jean-François Lyotard's *The Postmodern Condition* (1978). In this book, Lyotard claims that the 'grand narratives' of modernity have been 'delegitimated': after Auschwitz, great overarching stories like progress are revealed in all their implausibility. In postmodernity we inhabit only 'micronarratives', which are smaller in scale, more sensitive to the particularity and individuality.

Shopping and Fucking is a fast-moving play, the dialogue is kept short, the scenes are spare and witty, but this speech is given prominence through its placement in a kind of pause in the action and through its relative length. This might encourage us to treat it as Ravenhill's authorial intervention in the play, giving us the play's message. But we should remember that the speech is being spoken by a young man to his ex-boyfriend's new partner. In context it may be a rather crushing speech, designed to belittle Gary's desires, his place in their world. We have no obligation to think even that Robbie really believes it, let alone Ravenhill.

While the play depicts a world fragmented and broken, where there are no values that aren't economic values, it does not accept that world. As Ravenhill put it in an interview that coincided with the play's premiere: 'It's satirically swiping at a kind of moral and spiritual emptiness, where everything is defined in terms of consumption. The characters [...] are desperately trying to find a different set of values, but they can't' (quoted in Dominic Cavendish, 'On Theatre', *Independent*, 27 September 1996). Despite the saturation of the world of the play – and perhaps of our world – with the laws of economic exchange, the play returns again and again to the questions: what other values are there? Where can we find them?

The play does not ask these questions in the epic style of the 1970s and this is one of the reasons for the critical uncertainty that has surrounded it. In the absence of showpiece debates, an expansive historical scope, or a group of characters carefully located in their historical context, critics used to these devices as signifiers of the political play simply failed to recognise *Shopping and Fucking* as a political play at all.

Here *was* a political play but in a new mode and certainly the first of its elusive, ambiguous kind to break right into the mainstream. It was not however without precedent, though those precedents were mainly to be found not in the theatre but in the North American novel.

'Blank generation'

In the mid-nineties, searching for examples of writing that could capture the despairing moral nihilism of the world he saw around him, Mark Ravenhill alighted upon a group of novelists sometimes referred to as the 'blank generation' writers:

> the bored, drifting, drug-addled neurotics depicted by Jay McInerney, Douglas Coupland, and Dennis Cooper, depicted with irony and a submerged sense of moral disgust – damaged kids, damaging each other, damaging themselves, at sea without any sense of history, of politics, of society. These American writers didn't write about the working class or the underclass, but about middle-class kids whose life had no meaning, with an overwhelming death wish.
>
>   (Ravenhill, 'A Tear in the Fabric', p. 311)

This was a group of writers who emerged in the mid-to-late eighties and early nineties, an era when what was being championed in American literature was 'dirty realism', exemplified by writers like Raymond Carver, Richard Ford, and Tobias Wolff, who wrote plain, raw, small-scale, minor-key tragedies about ordinary people struggling to get by. In sharp contrast, the new generation was urban, post-punk, unflinchingly contemporary, and deeply immersed in a commercial culture by which they seemed in equal measure repelled and utterly seduced.

The term 'blank generation' was coined by two literary critics, Elizabeth Young and Graham Caveney, to describe this group, and in particular to pick out for attention 'the flat, stunned quality of much of the writing' (Young and Caveney, p. xiii). This 'strangely vacuous' tone – as Ravenhill once put it – is one of the most disturbing and intriguing features of their work. The most notorious example is Bret Easton Ellis's *American Psycho* (1991), a long, unremitting monologue by Patrick Bateman, a serial killer, whose various

unbearably savage murders are described in great detail, but with
virtually no emotional engagement. When he is not killing, Bateman
treats others with a kind of hyperconsumerist autism, listing in bland
detail the designer attire of everyone he meets:

> The three of us, Todd Hamlin and George Reeves and myself, are sitting in
> Harry's and it's a little after six. Hamlin is wearing a suit by Lubiam, a silk
> tie by Resikeio and a belt from Ralph Lauren. Reeves is wearing a six-
> button double-breasted suit by Christian Dior, a cotton shirt, a patterned
> silk tie by Claiborne, perforated cap-toe leather lace-ups by Allen Edmonds,
> a cotton handkerchief in his pocket, probably from Brooks Brothers;
> sunglasses by Lafont Paris lie on a napkin by his drink and a fairly nice
> attaché case from T. Anthony rests on an empty chair by our table. (p. 87)

. . . and so it goes on for almost 400 pages. The effect is numbing,
even boring, but that's the point. Ellis's prose style is trying to mimic
an outlook so sunk in consumerism that it sees other people merely as
objects in matrices of economic exchange; from there, the book
implies, it is only a short step to seeing others as objects who exist
purely for one's own pleasure, even if that pleasure includes
murdering them.

In the interview I quoted above, Ravenhill lamented that the
fragmentation of the theatre and its audience in the 1980s meant that
plays no longer talked to each other. The blank generation novels, on
the other hand, seem to be in constant contact. Patrick Bateman
works at Pierce and Pierce, the Wall Street firm that employed
Sherman McCoy from Tom Wolfe's *Bonfire of the Vanities* (1987)
and also makes deranged cameo appearances in Ellis's *Glamorama*
(1998), which is narrated by Victor Ward, who originally appeared in
Ellis's own *The Rules of Attraction* (1988), which also featured Sean
Bateman, Patrick's brother. In *Glamorama* we also find Alison Poole,
the anti-heroine of Jay McInerney's *Story of My Life* (1988). Patrick
seems to know someone called Stash, who might be the Stash of

Slaves of New York (1986), written by another of the blank
generation novelists, Tama Janowitz.

All of this might seem very incestuous but in fact it adds to the
complexity of these novels which mix their readily identifiable
cultural references (clothes, bars, movies, etc.) with an intriguing layer
of unreality. Ravenhill's plays often feature similar destabilising
references; his play *Handbag* (1998), for example, is a rewrite of
Oscar Wilde's *The Importance of Being Earnest* (1895), but also
features sly allusions to Martin Crimp's more contemporary plays
Dealing with Clair (1988) and *Getting Attention* (1991).

Incidents from these novels find themselves transformed and
scattered through Ravenhill's plays. And everywhere in the novels and
the plays is the same unmistakable tone of benumbed moral vacuity, a
disconnected, insensate shallowness that is its own condemnation; the
chorus member in Ravenhill's *Faust is Dead* (1997) who avers, 'I'm
the kind of person who can stand in the middle of an earthquake and
I'm just like "whoa, neat earthquake"' (*Plays: 1*, p. 137) is obviously
a distant relation of Alison Poole's friend Francesca whose ability to
make small talk is legendary: 'Granted, it's a little bit *too* much
sometimes – like, Francesca, I'd like you to meet Adolf Hitler, and
she'd be like – oh, wow, I just loved your last war' (McInerney, *Story
of My Life*, p. 20); or John in Dennis Cooper's *Closer* (1989) about
whom it is said, 'Here's a guy who'd watch newsreels of Nazi death
camps, then say something like, "Wow, this old black-and-white film
stock is *beautiful*"' (pp. 121–2).

Irony

It should not detract from *Shopping and Fucking*'s originality and
power to acknowledge its indebtedness to these earlier novels. Indeed
Ravenhill's play takes its place so confidently among them that
together they seem to illuminate each other, both through their

similarities and their differences. Like Ravenhill, the blank generation
novelists inspired some scepticism because of their swift rise to
cultural notoriety. The stubborn refusal of these authors in their
novels explicitly to condemn the shallow and arguably immoral lives
of their characters led to accusations of complicity. For example,
American Psycho's affectless prose initially confused the critics into
believing that Ellis must in some way be endorsing the vile murders he
depicted, and for a time he found himself the target of a brutal moral
crusade. Eventually Ellis had to make it clear: 'The acts described in
the book are truly, indisputably vile. The book is not. Patrick
Bateman is a monster. I am not' (quoted in Young and Caveney,
p. 86).

This clarification should not have been necessary had people read
the book attentively. Throughout the novel, a succession of tiny
ironies tilt it against Bateman, creating a clear discrepancy between
the book and its narrator. By the end, it becomes clear that these
horrific acts may even be fantasies in Bateman's head, though it is
ambiguous on this point. And the only light relief in this inescapable
vortex of a book comes in three short chapters in which Bateman
takes us through the highlights of his CD collection: the artists he
singles out for special praise, Genesis (post-Peter Gabriel), Huey
Lewis and the News, and Whitney Houston, would be recognised by
most readers as among the worst examples of air-brushed and
soulless, overproduced, empty corporate rock. Yet, ironically,
Bateman writes about them all with sincerity and passion – the only
time in the book that he engages with anything in that way. When he
writes of Whitney Houston that she is 'the most exciting and original
black jazz voice of her generation' (p. 256), the juxtaposition between
the tone of studious rock journalism and the joyless muzak about
which he is writing is hilarious, but in its own way chilling.

In *Shopping and Fucking*, it is precisely the same refusal to make
editorialising judgments that provides the initial moral challenge and

the same succession of sly ironies that encourages us to fill in the moral gaps in the picture. For although it is true that these characters seem content to be bereft of a sense of history, or of social responsibility, there are just occasionally hints that suggest a deeper dissatisfaction with the limitations of their lives.

In McInerney's *Story of My Life*, the book's narrator, Alison Poole, lives a life of casual sex, colossal drug use, and a complete refusal to take anything or anyone seriously. This makes for the book's readability, but the further one goes on through it, the more jarring does Alison's relentless upbeatness seem, as she becomes more and more tired and alienated. The book's title reappears throughout as a catchy refrain, usually there to punctuate some very minor misfortune in her life, though through its jangling repetition we cannot fail to notice that while the narrator refers to her life all the time, she never really seems to understand it. More and more often her sassy cynicism cracks and she admits her yearning for something perfect and sincere, as when she discusses true love:

> I say – what are you, soft in the head? It never lasts. I haven't seen one example yet. But there's still this ideal in your head, you know, like a vision of a place you've never visited, but that you've dreamed about or seen in a movie you've forgotten the title of, and you know you'd recognize it immediately if you ever saw it in real life. It would be like going home, tied and whipped after a really long time on the road. (p. 33)

Similarly, in Douglas Coupland's *Microserfs* (1995), the narrator's devotion to the software company to whom he appears to have given his entire working life is rarely challenged, except for a few double pages which are taken over by a kind of digital screaming, pages of apparently meaningless machine code, that suggest an eruption of unconscious resistance to a life of corporate slavery.

In *Shopping and Fucking*, characters occasionally give voice to similar, barely intended insights. Mark has been encouraged to believe that his desire for human affection is a kind of craven addiction of which he has to be cured. He returns from a clinic parroting a therapeutic vocabulary of 'emotional dependencies' that he has to 'work through' (p. 17). He tries to use economic exchange to neutralise his desire for others – 'I thought if I pay then it won't mean anything' (p. 25). But the play continues to keep open the thought that perhaps his desire for others is not the pathological state that his therapists appear to believe, and his confession to Gary is compelling because it is so unadorned, 'Now, here, when you're with me I feel like a person and if you're not with me I feel less like a person' (pp. 55–6).

There is also the matter of the characters' names. Robbie, Mark and Gary in *Shopping and Fucking* are named after various members of the 1990s boy band Take That. And remember that one of their biggest hits had Lulu as guest vocalist. Brian, meanwhile, is perhaps appropriately named after the ugly leader of the rival gang, Brian Harvey from East 17. At one level, it's a throwaway cultural reference; originally there were more characters in the play, but Howard and Jason prophetically disappeared during rewrites. But the choice of names points up the deliberate thinness of characterisation. Their names reinforce the sense that these are characters without fully-realised, naturalistic pasts. Further, it suggests a life entirely colonised by commercial culture.

In Dennis Cooper's *Closer*, one chapter presents the character of David, a boy whose fantasies of being a teen pop idol are so vivid he appears to have convinced himself they are real. However, he hasn't just taken on the image, but also the worthlessness and contempt attached to that image. He opens his monologue with the words, 'I'm a talentless but popular young singer and I have the feeling someone is watching me. I use the term loosely because I have few feelings, and even they're too simple, like primary colours' (p. 21). By identifying with the despised image, David has taken the shallowness and artificiality of that image into himself. This is perhaps a commentary on the way mass culture can colonise the very imaginations of those who immerse themselves in it. As the German cultural theorist Theodor Adorno wrote, 'Talented performers belong to the system long before it displays them' (*Dialectic of Enlightenment*, trs. John Cumming, London, Allen Lane, 1973, p. 122). A way of understanding what he means here is to think of the contestants on shows like *Pop Idol*: the show does not groom them for anodyne pop stardom; they've done it themselves, in their bedrooms, practising singing, dancing, dressing like their heroes, taking those banal images into themselves. The simple act of naming the characters draws close attention to the banalising effects of mass culture and the possible misfit between the person and their identity.

In a more dramatic moment, Robbie recalls the epiphany he experiences rushing off the effect of four E:

> I was looking down on this planet. Spaceman over this earth. And I see this kid in Rwanda, crying, but he doesn't know why. And this granny in Kiev, selling everything she's ever owned. And this president in Bogota or . . . South America. And I see the suffering. And the wars. And the grab, grab, grab.
>
> And I think: Fuck Money. Fuck it. This selling. This buying. This system. Fuck the bitching world and let's be . . . beautiful. Beautiful. And happy.
>
> (p. 39)

It's a finely balanced speech. On the one hand, we're laughing at his chemically-induced reverie, the absurd naivety of his insight, but on the other, we recognise the resonance of his claim. Many of the problems that emerge in the play would be solved if it were possible to 'Fuck it. This selling. This buying'. His perspective finds echoes throughout the play: in Brian's sudden yearning for Edenic purity as he watches a video of his son playing the cello and in Lulu's enthusiastic advocacy of the microwave meals that she's shoplifted, which offer a similar, if politically ambiguous, global vision: 'you've got the world here. You've got all the tastes in the world. You've got an empire under cellophane. Look, China. India. Indonesia. In the past you'd have to invade, you'd have to occupy just to get one of these things' (p. 61).

Robbie's speech was slightly rewritten during the first rehearsals, as a comparison between the first and second editions of the play reveals. In the first version, he saw simply 'this kid in Rwanda. And this granny in Kiev. And this president in Bogota or . . .' (*Shopping and Fucking*, London, Methuen, 1996, p. 38). The rewrite sharpens the sense that his insight is that across the world people are unable to understand their own suffering; it's a perspective somewhat akin to the reader of *Story of My Life* who understands before the narrator does the real story of her life. It also forms a link with Lulu – like Alison Poole, a would-be actress – who offers as her shopping-channel audition speech Irina's lament at the end of Chekhov's *Three Sisters* (1901), 'One day people will know what all this is for. All this suffering. There'll be no more mysteries. But until then we have to carry on living. We must work. That's all we can do' (p. 13). Unfortunately, as the play suggests, this day of perfect self-awareness is still a long way off.

Fathers

Just as the characters in *Shopping and Fucking* seem to lack jobs, families, histories, it's striking how often the novels of the blank generation centre on young people without parents. There's a haunting scene in Bret Easton Ellis's first novel, *Less Than Zero* (1985), in which the book's protagonist, Clay, visits his parental home, and it is pristinely empty, as if his mum and dad were just figments of his imagination.

Perhaps what this attempts to capture is the disjunction between those who lived through the sixties – that era, as we've seen, of radicalism, utopianism and political opposition – and those born after it who grew up in the Reagan/Thatcher era. This is one of the central strands of Douglas Coupland's *Shampoo Planet* (1992), whose narrator, Tyler, is a Reaganite entrepreneur with nothing but affectionate contempt for the other-worldly values of his ex-hippy mother. It's a theme that Ravenhill will explore more directly in 1999's *Some Explicit Polaroids*.

This generational clash seems to stand for a political clash, between old radicals and young conservatives. The parents stand for sixties-style paternalism, the children for consumerism and the market. Yet the battle lines are blurred in these books. Alison Poole is certainly a Reaganite individualist (if she were the sort of person to permit labels of this kind), but one of the slips in the book is her desire for her father to behave like a father:

> I call Dad but of course there's no answer there. I'm such a sucker – every time I dial him I can't help getting this little tingle of hope. It's a miracle if I can even find him, but I sort of fantasize that he'll pick up the phone some day and say, is that you, Alison? I love you, honey, and I'm really sorry about the last fifteen years or so, I don't know what came over me but I'm better now and I'm so sorry . . . (p. 81)

This is despite a murky series of connections in the book between the poisoning of her favourite horse, her childhood experience of being raped by a stablehand, and her father's complicity in both acts.

Later in the book, Alison goes to see August Wilson's play *Fences* which features a scene in which a son spits in his father's face. She finds the moment electrifying – to the exclusion of anything else in the play. Her same ambivalence about fathers appears when she observes of James Earl Jones, the actor playing him: 'That guy's so powerful he's like the ultimate father where you can't tell if he's God or Satan or what' (p. 97).

Fathers occupy a similarly ambivalent role in *Shopping and Fucking*. Brian's paternal affection for his son seems vaguely heartfelt and it connects with the bemusingly idealised image of fatherhood in *The Lion King*, a film that acts as a comic counterpoint to many of the play's themes. But Gary's story is altogether more troubling. With Mark he implies that he was being abused by his stepfather before he left home yet his imagined ideal partner seems to have the same sexualised mixture of protection and violence: 'I want to be owned. I want someone to look after me. And I want him to fuck me. Really fuck me. Not like that, not like him. And, yeah, it'll hurt. But a good hurt' (p. 56).

At the climax of the play, Gary pays Mark, Robbie and Lulu to take him through a role-play which will end with him being fucked to death by his father. There is something of Alison Poole's indecision in this image of the father: all-powerful like God but, in Gary's desire to be penetrated by a knife or a screwdriver, a distant recollection of the mythic imagery of the devil's flint penis. In Dennis Cooper's *Closer*, George speculates:

> if God made a visit to earth it'd be in the form of a kiss. Being kissed by someone I admire is the closest I've gotten to peace on earth, like Xmas carolers sing. God would give each boy a taste of His lips then go back to whatever dimension He hides in. (p. 47)

Entirely characteristic of all these works is the juxtaposition of perfect kindness with sexual defilement. Equally telling is the final recognition that God the Father nowadays mostly seems to be hiding away somewhere. But why this ambivalence, what is being expressed through this repeated motif of the sexual father?

There's an echo of Robbie's speech about 'little stories' in Douglas Coupland's *Generation X* (1991), when Dag declares: 'I'm just upset that the world has gotten too big – way beyond our capacity to tell stories about it, and so all we're stuck with are these blips and chunks and snippets on bumpers' (p. 5). However, Coupland's characters persist, telling each other stories undaunted, because, as Claire remarks, 'either our lives become stories, or there's just no way to get through them' (p. 8). Later in the novel, they are referred to as 'bedtime stories', and perhaps once again we are feeling the ambivalent trace of the absent father. In Mark's repeated story of buying Robbie and Lulu there is a similar ambiguity between paternalism and predation.

What is at stake in this motif of fatherhood is a transformation of the social ambiguity of the paternal role, transformed into a deep political ambiguity. In our culture conventional family roles require fathers to be both unconditionally protective and firmly disciplinarian. In *Shopping and Fucking*, as in the novels, the father who is missing is the protective father, the father from the sixties, the paternalist, welfare father; the father who appears in these books is the disciplinarian, but now without the protective instinct. Through the character of Brian we can see what this father correlates to: money. His own father told him that 'Get. The Money. First' were the first words in the Bible (p. 87) and he tells Robbie that behind everything 'behind beauty, behind God, behind paradise', even behind the father, is 'money' (p. 48). Perhaps this father that will kill us all is the unfettered force of capital, the unrestrained force of consumerism.

Violence and the body

One of the things that characterises *Shopping and Fucking* and several other plays from the mid-nineties – like much of Sarah Kane's work – is a determination to present sexual acts and violence on stage without coyness or sentiment. These are sometimes referred to as shock-effects, though this is a phrase that should be used with care. 'I've never had the desire to shock,' remarks Ravenhill. 'It's a boring desire and I think you'd write really badly if you woke up in the morning and said, "Today I'm going to try to shock somebody." I have shocked myself a bit but I had to be true to what the characters demanded' (Janie Lawrence, 'The Shock of the New Ravenhill', *The Times* (Arts Supplement), 7 July 2003, p. 14). It might be better to understand these images in terms of Bret Easton Ellis's belief that 'only the most extreme and disruptive images or experiences can penetrate the bland vacuity of his generation' (Young and Caveney, p. 93).

One of the most profound and unsettling meditations on the contemporary body is Dennis Cooper's novel, *Closer*. The central figure is George Miles, a boy whose extreme sexual passivity seems to blur the line between life and death. (He is undoubtedly one of the sources for Gary in *Shopping and Fucking*.) What is unsettling in the novel is the rigorous way in which this idea is developed. There is something uncanny about George's corpse-like behaviour during sex; Cliff recalls: 'The night we fucked [. . .] I had this weird feeling I was alone and not alone at the same time' (p. 84). The experience asks the question, what is the difference between being alive and being dead? In that sense, what is another person? Their body? Their soul? (Does such a thing exist?) In one wholly chilling sequence, a group of men who have the fantasy of killing a beautiful boy during sex watch a snuff movie in which this takes place. They ask the film's maker to tell them when the boy dies: 'At what seemed a haphazard point, everyone in the room heard a brief, curt announcement. "Now," it said. Philippe knew that word, but he hadn't realized what it meant at first' (p. 109). Because what is that moment *between* life and death? What can that 'now' mean?

These questions are also at work in *Shopping and Fucking*, though in a less intense form. For Mark, as we have seen, money acts as a kind of anaesthetic, a barrier that softens the impact of the world on us and of us on the world. In a society where money has become the dominant value, we live our lives in a permanently desensitised state.

At various points in the play, the body's leaky instability comes to represent both the promise and the danger of breaking through that anaesthetic haze and renewing our numbed sensations. It's a positive thing to Brian, when he discovers a tear, and describes it as a 'little drop of pure emotion' (p. 45). However, for Mark, shocked to discover blood in his mouth after rimming Gary (p. 26), or Lulu's horrified reaction to finding some on her face (pp. 27–8), blood is an untidy reminder that other people cannot easily be commodified. As such the body may appear to be a site of resistance to capital.

However, even this uncertain claim is undermined in the final scene when Gary's fate is hinted at only in Robbie's line (added in rehearsal) 'You've got a bit of blood' (p. 90). Whether they wipe it away or leave it, the blood suggests the ultimate triumph of capital over the body.

From 'gay' to 'queer'

Dennis Cooper's novel has something else in common with *Shopping and Fucking*: none of the characters ever define themselves sexually. There are no 'coming-out' speeches; barely anyone uses the word 'gay'; as in *Less Than Zero*, the characters seem to be, if anything, casually bisexual. Both works are responding to – indeed are part of – a shift in gay culture and politics that took place from the mid-1980s and help explain the originality of Ravenhill's play.

The Gay Liberation Front that emerged in the late sixties was originally infused with the radical politics of the counter-culture, the civil rights movement, and the strategic imagination of the situationists. Their campaigns were flamboyant, involving direct action 'zaps' and the reclaiming of once-denigrated images of homosexuality like drag and effeminacy. The GLF collapsed in 1972 and its place at the heart of the emergent gay politics was taken by the Campaign for Homosexual Equality. This was a far less radical

organisation, emerging from reformist rather than revolutionary
political traditions. Under the leadership of the CHE, gay politics
insisted that lesbians and gay men represented no threat to
heterosexual culture, because 'we're all the same'. Sissies, butch
dykes, drag queens and other such 'negative' images tended to be
discouraged as distracting from this assimilationist message.
Correspondingly, the political campaigns aimed to extend to lesbians
and gay men the same rights as were available to straights: the right
to marry, for example, to join the army, and an equal age of consent.

While some important rights were secured in this way, the problem
with trying to model your identity on heterosexuality is that if
heterosexual society turns against you, you have deprived yourself of
any independent sources of strength. Indeed, in the 1980s, the new
right-wing governments in Britain and America were unsympathetic
to the gay cause, with literally lethal consequences. The arrival of
AIDS in San Francisco in the early eighties was met with indifference
by the Reagan presidency and a frank refusal to publicise the virtues
of safe sex or to support medical research that might have found ways
to slow the spread of infection. In Britain, the government also
dragged its feet on the issue of gay men's health and indeed enacted,
in 1988, the era's most directly oppressive piece of anti-gay
legislation: section 28 of the Local Government Act, which forbade
Local Authorities from spending any money to 'promote
homosexuality'. This might have included funding gay theatre
companies, gay refuges for victims of domestic violence, lesbian and
gay social events, even libraries stocking copies of Plato's *Symposium*.
Schools were funded through the Local Authority and the act
specifically forbade teachers from suggesting that 'pretended family
relationships' were on any kind of equal moral footing to
heterosexual ones.

In response, a new wave of political activists looked back to the
early years of GLF to create renewed forms of political intervention.

In March 1987, ACT-UP (the AIDS Coalition To Unleash Power) held its first demonstration on Wall Street, in protest against the Food and Drugs Administration refusing to act to reduce the cost of AZT, which was at the time the most effective treatment for symptoms of HIV infection. For several hours, 250 activists handed out leaflets and brought traffic to a standstill. Three years later, the organisation widened its focus to broader issues of gay politics, leading to the formation of Queer Nation in the summer of 1990. Inspired by ACT-UP, OutRage! followed in May 1990, disrupting homophobic events like the Congress of the Family, taking peaceful but disruptive direct action against (then) gay-hostile companies like Texaco and Benetton. They held queer weddings and kiss-ins to protest against gay invisibility. In 1992, Sarah Schulman and others formed the Lesbian Avengers who were famous for their slogans ('We want revenge and we want it now!' 'We recruit!') and for their spectacular fire-eating. On a similar level of high theatricality, the Sisters of Perpetual Indulgence, a group of gay male nuns with outrageously suggestive names, was officially convened in 1980 and a British chapter in 1990.

Along with this went a shift of usage from 'gay' to 'queer'. Gay was felt to be too soft, too implicated in the reformism of the CHE, and instead activists decided to reclaim the word queer. It suggested an assertion of difference, not a desire to assimilate; it suggested a slanted viewpoint, a unique perspective that was outside the mainstream; it demonstrated the outsiderliness, and the refusal to integrate.

Queer politics had an immediate cultural impact. The early nineties saw the emergence of 'New Queer Cinema' with films like Todd Haynes's *Poison* (1991), Tom Kalin's *Swoon* (1992), and Gregg Araki's *The Living End* (1992) and *Totally Fucked Up* (1993). (This last film – which depicts a group of aimless young queers talking to camera about their angst-ridden lives and otherwise hanging out – was an influence on Ravenhill when he was writing *Shopping and*

Fucking.) What makes these films distinctively queer rather than gay is their refusal to explain homosexuality, to treat it as a problem, to apologise for it, even to name it.

The legitimate theatre took longer to respond to queer, though theatre artists like Neil Bartlett were already mixing a high-art aesthetic with the culture of the drag bar in the late eighties. Many gay plays still had earnest coming-out scenes, positive images, heart-warming endings and an absence of any difficult political subjects. An exemplary 'gay' play would be Jonathan Harvey's *Beautiful Thing* (1993) which follows the burgeoning love between two boys on a council estate. It's an accomplished and attractive play but the political rough edges of gay experience in Britain have been carefully smoothed away.

Queer theatre

A more daring approach is taken by Canadian writer Brad Fraser in his play *Unidentified Human Remains and the True Nature of Love* (1989). It follows a gay man, David, and his female friend, Candy, as he negotiates a new relationship and she dispenses with her old one. In the background of the story of them and their friends, however, is the story of a serial killer at loose in their community. Eventually they discover that he is one of their friends and they confront him in the penultimate scene.

The play is as queer as *Beautiful Thing* is gay. The intertwining of homosexuality and murder was just the sort of negative association that the CHE campaigners would have run a mile from. The sexuality of the characters isn't made clear and doesn't have to be, a comfortable and casual bisexuality settles over the proceedings. References to the characters' sexuality are usually brushed jokingly aside . . .

Kane You're gay huh?

David Not professionally. (p. 56)

. . . and heterosexual anxieties about queers are dismissed with amused contempt:

Jerri Some people are freaked out by gays.

Candy Some people like polyester. (p. 87)

The play strikes some familiar chords. As Brad Fraser admitted, 'I wanted my characters to operate in the here and now and refer to the past even less than we do in real life' (p. 5), just as Ravenhill aimed to strike all but wholly contemporary references from his play. The two plays share a younger man with an implied sexual fixation on his father; both plays mix sex and murder; and both kill off a character in the gap between the penultimate and the final scene.

Ravenhill has identified himself as a queer – rather than a gay – playwright and he shows a characteristically mischievous desire to overturn some of the pieties of 'gay' politics. 'Gay people have had enough positive images,' he once declared. 'What those nellies need is some negative images to shake them up.' In similar vein, he differentiated the values of his work from the values of the annual 'Gay Pride' event: 'I introduced gay shame into theatre!' (http://newyorkmetro/nymetro/arts/features/2160).

His play features no 'coming-out' speeches, it is entirely silent about AIDS (though the fear of bodily fluids may have an echo of that crisis), or any other of the major political campaigns. It unflatteringly contrasts Brian's earnest affirmation of the traditional family with Mark, Lulu, and Robbie's alternative 'pretended family relationship'. And rather like OutRage! storming Westminster Cathedral during a service, there was something awfully queer about *Shopping and Fucking*'s success in the West End.

Shopping and fucking

The two terms in the play's title bring together the two political strands on which it draws: an examination of the consumer society and a sensitivity to the dynamics of contemporary relationships. And the two terms couple promiscuously through the play, creating new permutations in almost every scene: a blow job in a Harvey Nichols changing room, Lulu going topless in an audition for a shopping channel, Mark's attempt to turn his desires into transactions, Gary paying for a sexual role-play scenario, phone sex, rent boys, and so on. The play continues to find new combinations of these fundamental social acts.

Sex has been used to make money for hundreds of years, of course. Nonetheless, in the 1980s, the feminist argument that using women's bodies to sell products was degrading and insulting did appear to have been listened to. But in the 1990s, perhaps as part of capitalism's new global triumphalism, this was abandoned and advertisers were back to their old tricks. Eroticism, nudity, the promise of sexual satisfaction, almost always involving the exploitation of women's bodies, were once again the staples of the advertiser's art. Products with no conceivable erotic charge were sold with sex. In one particularly desperate moment, the advertisers of Microsoft's Encarta Encyclopedia tried to attract sales with the slogan 'Covers Everything', illustrated with a woman holding an open copy of the book over her breasts. Such desperate acts were amusing in isolation, grotesque taken as a whole, and they remind us that the myriad permutations of fucking and shopping in *Shopping and Fucking* reflect in a fairly precise way the fate of desire under capitalism.

The two terms are not, however, identical; they do not lose their meanings, however much capital tries to turn fucking into just another kind of shopping. The play continually reminds us that money is a poor prophylactic for desire, that no matter how hard capitalism may threaten to turn all encounters into economic transactions, our need for love can never be fully expressed in economic terms. Mark's psychobabble is, after all, a subject for sad satire, and despite the persuasive consumerism, there are chinks in the smooth surface, in which a character will unwittingly reveal a desire for something beyond shopping. As Robbie discovers in the burger bar, one of the weaknesses of the free-market argument is that sometimes people just don't want choice.

As a theatrical experience too, the play is artfully designed to produce a sense of artistic completeness and wholeness, a patterning across the surface of the performance, that exceeds the individual characters' understanding of their lives. The repeated motifs – shopping combined with fucking, fatherhood, security cameras, blood, individual portions, etc. – signal to each other across the play, drawing our attention to the larger structure of the piece. In a sense, artistically, the play offers us the kind of perspective that Robbie achieves only with the help of four E. We take in the whole play, understanding the place of all the characters in a way that is unavailable to them. This is the source of the play's political sophistication: its compassionate irony, its structural beauty, and the perspective it affords all combine to ask us to imagine a world without buying and selling.

Production history

Shopping and Fucking was Mark Ravenhill's first full-length play. He'd written a couple of short plays which had attracted the attention of Max Stafford-Clark, the erstwhile artistic director of the Royal Court, co-founder of the seminal 1970s touring theatre group, Joint Stock, and latterly the co-founder and artistic director of Out of Joint. Stafford-Clark has had a long history of working with new writers and after seeing *Fist* at the Finborough Theatre, London, in December 1994, he asked if Ravenhill had anything else to show him. Ravenhill didn't, but he claimed he did, writing a first draft of what would become *Shopping and Fucking* in a couple of months.

The original title was *Fucking Diana* and concerned someone making a pornographic film with a Princess Diana lookalike. (This idea only exists vestigially in Mark's story from Scene Thirteen of the current version.) But the play developed no doubt in part through the influence of the blank generation novels he'd been reading and the plays by Brad Fraser, Martin Crimp, Anthony Nielson, and others. A key component was the title which came from an encounter with a colleague who told the story of shocking an old schoolfriend by telling her 'Oh, I'm writing a shopping and fucking novel' (Sierz, p. 123).

After going through a number of drafts with Max Stafford-Clark, in June 1996 director, writer and actors took two weeks at the National Theatre Studio to workshop the script, which changed as the actors, under Stafford-Clark's direction, researched and questioned their characters. During this workshop Anthony Ryding, playing Gary, realised that it would make a lot of sense for his character to be a rent boy. Further rewrites continued through the summer and smaller alterations were worked out during the rehearsal period and the show opened on 1 October 1996 at the Royal Court Theatre Upstairs at the Ambassadors Theatre. Inauspiciously, the performance began after 9.00 to leave the way clear for Harold Pinter's new play, *Ashes to Ashes*. The Theatre Upstairs was a small space, seating an audience of only sixty.

Max Stafford-Clark is knows for his detailed textual work, taking his actors and his writer through a challenging investigation of every line of the play. Since the production was researched and developed with the same cast, that added a degree of authenticity to the performances that was acknowledged in more than one review.

Stafford-Clark was particularly keen to give definition to the
characters by locating their archetypal qualities, finding a subtle level
of almost mythical resonance to this story. Bad fathers, good fathers,
hero and mother: identifying this kept the play clear, added a weight
and stature to the characters, and brought out more strongly what the
play was about.

The play was performed on an almost bare stage with only
rudimentary furniture; the most striking element of the set was a
series of neon signs attached to the rear wall; between scenes these
signs would flash on and off, eventually settling on a word – such as
'Home', 'Bedsit', 'Money', 'Sweet' – that would remain in the
background through a scene, sometimes lighting up to emphasise a
particular moment, as when Brian opens his briefcase in Scene Two to
show Lulu what he wants her to sell. Wittily, the letter 'E' was
suddenly illuminated on the back wall.

Between scenes, they chose the 1994 club anthem 'Cantgetaman,
Cantgetajob (Life's a Bitch)' by Sister Bliss featuring Collette (Go-Beat,
October 1994). Apart from locating the production precisely within a
faintly campy urban environment, the track's series of nervous clashing
chords strung over a powerful squelching bass line emphasised the
restless discontent of the song's lyrics, spoken over the top with diva-
ish relish: 'I can't pay no *bills* / I can't walk my *dog* / I can't get a *man*'.

The original production was generally well received at the Royal
Court and, following an English regional tour, it returned to the
Royal Court for a second run in January 1997 before heading off on
another tour. In June 1997, the production transferred to the Gielgud
Theatre in London's West End. It was at this point that the play's title
started attracting so much attention. A number of archaic laws meant
that the play's full title could not be spoken on the telephone by the
box office staff (unless the customer spoke the offending word first);
the playtext (just like this one) could not print the word on its cover
and ways had to be found for it to be artfully concealed from the

casual bookshop browser; the posters were the same, but even in their asterisked form, London Underground refused to allow their poster-sites to be used; after legal advice, Newman Display, the company hired to put up the neon signage outside the theatre withdrew their services; one member of the new cast, Robert Portal, walked out on the production claiming that his role (Mark) was 'morally repugnant', which rather poses the question whether he'd read it before accepting the job; the mailing house used to send out the leaflets complained about the title, and according to one of the show's producers, Guy Chapman, 'we have even had ladies with umbrellas ripping down the signs. We think it's fun.'

Critics were split on the West End revival. Some felt that it lost something in the transfer from the intimate Theatre Upstairs to the more cavernous Gielgud. Others felt the play grew in resonance and maturity in the larger space. Nonetheless the production did good business for the whole of its six-week run. The following year the play returned to the West End again, this time to the Queen's Theatre next door, for a longer, four-month stay. Another version of the same production meanwhile toured, including a brief showing at the Euro Theatre '98 festival in Brussels. This was also the subject of controversy when the Education Secretary, David Blunkett, heard that the play was receiving British Council funding.

> The play was full of unacceptable foul language and apparently designed to shock: 'Shakespeare didn't need that, did he?. . . We don't want to shock all the time. We should be creating a society of civilised human beings by teaching democracy, citizenship, and moral and spiritual values.
>
> 'I've no idea how much the British Council is spending on supporting this tour; but if it's a penny, it's a penny too much . . . I don't think it is a good example of the best of British.'
>
> (Stephen Bates, 'Ministers in culture clash as drama upsets Blunkett', *Guardian*, 24 March 1998, p. 9)

Despite this, the play was a considerable success in Europe where productions began to appear with great regularity. One of the most acclaimed was young German director Thomas Ostermeier's production at the Baracke at the Deutsches Theater, Berlin, in January 1998. This play – along with pieces by Sarah Kane and others – had a significant influence on a new wave of German theatremakers who acclaimed what they described, rather indelicately, as the 'blood and sperm' generation.

The play made converts and courted controversy wherever it appeared. In Israel the title was left untranslated in deference to local sensibilities; in Russia the more explicit acts were removed and all of the sexual language remained in English, even though the translator claimed, somewhat implausibly, that 'it would have been ideal for Stanislavsky – it's highly realistic'. At the beginning of September 1997, worrying about audience reaction, the British touring cast made a small change to Scene Thirteen, introducing Fergie in the toilet story before Diana. The real Diana had just been killed in Paris a few days earlier.

Shopping and Fucking, which began playing to sixty people a night at 9.00 in the evening, has had its performance rights bought in something like forty countries. It remains one of the key texts of the mid-nineties flowering of new British playwriting.

Further Reading

Plays by Mark Ravenhill

Plays: One, London, Methuen, 2001 (contains *Shopping and Fucking, Faust is Dead, Handbag, Some Explicit Polaroids*)

A Desire to Kill on the Tip of the Tongue [a translation from the French of *Un envie de tuer sur le bout de la langue* by Xavier Durringer] in David Bradby (ed.), *Frontline Drama 6: The French Issue*, London, Methuen, 1998

Sleeping Around (with Hilary Fannin, Stephen Greenhorn, and Abi Morgan), London, Methuen, 1998

Mother Clap's Molly House (with Matthew Scott), London, Methuen, 2001

Totally Over You, in *Shell Connections 2003: New Plays for Young People*, London, Faber and Faber, 2003

Other writing by Ravenhill

'Telly is rubbish. Politics is boring. And directors are b*******s', *Guardian*, 11 June 1997. [Comic account of a writers' symposium in Sweden, published on the eve of the West End opening of *Shopping and Fucking*.]

'My life was a voyage with Dr Who. Then the Tardis turned to cardboard', *Independent*, 27 January 1998. [Discusses his childhood fascination with *Doctor Who*, drawing comparisons with *Shopping and Fucking* in the depiction of a rootless pseudo-family constantly faced with dangerous worlds.]

'The bland national', *Guardian*, 30 May 1999. [Comparing British and American theatre institutions.]

'Help! I'm having an art attack!', *Guardian*, 18 November 2000. [Mischievously proposing a year-long moratorium on creativity to save us from cultural overload.]

'The bottom line', *Guardian*, 20 June 2001. [Probing the British theatre's current fascination with depictions of anal sex.]

'Almost famous', *Guardian*, 2 February 2002. [On the occasion of *Mother Clap's Molly House* transferring to the West End, Ravenhill discusses with fellow playwrights, Joe Penhall, Patrick Marber, and Charlotte Jones, the ingredients for a commercial hit.]

'A touch of evil', *Guardian*, 22 March 2003. [Exploring why British theatre and culture is so averse to metaphysics when, he suggests, the sources of creativity may themselves be mysteriously non-material.]

'Freak show', *Guardian*, 15 July 2003. [Coinciding with the performance of *Totally Over You* at the National Theatre, he discusses the experience of seeing the play performed by school groups.]

'That's entertainment?', *Guardian*, 4 December 2003. [A tribute to the joys of the seasonal pantomime.]

'*The Mother* by Bertolt Brecht', *Guardian*, 16 June 2004. [Published to coincide with a rehearsed reading that he directed at the Royal Court, Ravenhill considers the unfashionable political charms of Brecht's play.]

'I want to stay pure', *Guardian*, 26 August 2004. [Interview with fellow playwright, Anthony Neilson.]

'Kids – run for your lives!', *Guardian*, 15 September 2004. [Detects an illiberal equation of homosexuality and paedophilia in the new casting of the West End musical, *Chitty Chitty Bang Bang*.]

'A Tear in the Fabric: The Jamie Bulger Murder and New Theatre

Writing in the 'Nineties', *New Theatre Quarterly*, xx, 4 (NTQ 80)
(November 2004), pp. 305–14. [Considers the influence of the
murder of Jamie Bulger in 1993 on his own writing and general
cultural attitudes towards morality and the concept of evil.]
'"Surely this is a bit poofy?"', *Guardian*, 24 January 2005.
[Discussing the sexual dynamics of men playing women on stage.]
'Me, My iBook, and Writing in America', *Contemporary Theatre
Review*, 15. 3 (August 2005). [Discusses attempts to resist the
pervasive effect of American narratives on his own writing and the
complexities of writing about global politics.]

All of Ravenhill's contributions to the *Guardian* newspaper can be
accessed through the *Guardian*'s website: http://www.guardian.co.uk.

Writing about Ravenhill

William C. Boles, 'Violence at the Royal Court: Martin McDonagh's
The Beauty Queen of Leenane and Mark Ravenhill's *Shopping and
Fucking*', *Theatre Symposium: A Journal of the Southeastern
Theatre Conference*, 7 (1999), pp. 125–35.
Jonathan Croall, *Inside the Molly House: The National Theatre at
Work*, London, National Theatre, 2001. [Insider account of the
production process for Ravenhill's fifth major play, *Mother Clap's
Molly House*.]
Baz Kershaw, 'Oh for Unruly Audiences! Or, Patterns of Participation
in Twentieth-Century Theatre', *Modern Drama*, xliv, 2 (2001), pp.
133–54. [Within a very interesting discussion of the changing
patterns of British theatre audience behaviour, the essay touches on
the reception of *Shopping and Fucking* (especially Scene Thirteen)
in the immediate aftermath of Princess Diana's death.]
Aleks Sierz, *In-Yer-Face Theatre: British Drama Today*, London,
Faber and Faber, 2001. [A very influential reading of the new

generation of British playwrights that emerged in the mid-1990s and contains a substantial chapter on Ravenhill.]

Caridad Svich, 'Commerce and Morality in the Theatre of Mark Ravenhill', *Contemporary Theatre Review*, xiii, 1 (2003), pp. 81–95. [A good overview of Ravenhill's work up to *Mother Clap's Molly House*, with some sharp and provocative comments on the visual style of *Shopping and Fucking*.]

Merle Tönnies, 'Problematic Youth Identities in Contemporary British Drama', *Anglistik & Englischunterricht 6: Youth Identities: Teens and Tweens in British Culture*, ed. Hans-Jürgen Diller, Erwin Otto and Gerd Stratmann, Heidelberg, Universitätsverlag C., Winter 2000, pp. 107–23. [Sociologically-inclined analysis that considers *Shopping and Fucking* alongside two plays by playwrights of an earlier generation, *Class Enemy* by Nigel Williams and *Road* by Jim Cartwright.]

Leslie A. Wade, 'Postmodern Violence and Human Solidarity: Sex and Forks in *Shopping and Fucking*', *Theatre Symposium: A Journal of the Southeastern Theatre Conference*, 7 (1999), pp. 109–15. [Thoughtful analysis of the moral force of the violence in Ravenhill's play.]

For information on the earlier generation of political playwrights that Ravenhill is partly indebted to and partly reacting against, the following books are very useful:

Peter Ansorge, *Disrupting the Spectacle: Five Years of Experimental and Fringe Theatre in Britain*, London, Pitman, 1975

John Bull, *New British Political Dramatists*, London, Macmillan, 1984

Colin Chambers and Mike Prior, *Playwright's Progress: Patterns of Postwar Drama*, Oxford, Amber Lane, 1987

Catherine Itzin, *Stages in the Revolution: Political Theatre in Britain Since 1968*, London, Methuen, 1980

Simon Trussler, *New Theatre Voices of the Seventies: Sixteen Interviews from Theatre Quarterly 1970–1980*, London, Methuen, 1981

The following books are useful for background on contemporary British drama and contain sections on Ravenhill's work.

Dominic Dromgoole, *The Full Room: An A–Z of Contemporary Playwriting*, 2nd ed., London, Methuen, 2002, pp. 235–8. [Short but pertinent article on Ravenhill's work situating him within a tradition of British theatrical moral criticism.]

David Edgar, *State of Play: Playwrights on Playwriting*, London, Faber and Faber, 1999. [Contains a short talk by Ravenhill (pp. 48–51) about his relation to the disavowal of homosexuality that some say took place in British theatre in the 1950s. The introduction is an excellent outline of various trends in British drama during the 1990s.]

David Ian Rabey, *English Drama Since 1940*, London, Longman, 2003. [Contains a short but illuminating overview of Ravenhill's work up to *Some Explicit Polaroids* (pp. 201–4).]

Dominic Shellard, *British Theatre since the War*, New Haven and London, Yale University Press, 1999. [Contains only scattered reference to Ravenhill but is a very useful one-volume account of fifty years of British theatre.]

Influences

Ravenhill's dramaturgy draws on a number of examples and all of the following would illuminate the style of *Shopping and Fucking*.

David Mamet, *Edmond*, London, Methuen, 2003

Martin Crimp, *Dealing with Clair*, in *Plays: 1*, London, Faber and Faber, 2000

——, *No One Sees the Video*, in *Getting Attention: Two Plays and a Fiction*, London, Nick Hern Books, 1991

Brad Fraser, *Unidentified Human Remains and the True Nature of Love*, Edmonton, NeWest Press, 1996

Jonathan Harvey, *Beautiful Thing*, London, Methuen, 1996

The 'blank generation' novels provided an important key to discovering the moral tone of *Shopping and Fucking* and many threads can be traced between the play and these books.

Dennis Cooper, *Frisk,* London, Serpent's Tail, 1992

——, *Closer*, London, Serpent's Tail, 1994

Douglas Coupland, *Generation X: Tales For an Accelerated Culture*, London, Abacus, 1992

——, *Shampoo Planet*, London, Scribner, 1992

Bret Easton Ellis, *Less Than Zero*, London, Picador, 1986

——, *American Psycho*, London, Picador, 2000

Jay McInerney, *Story of My Life*, London, Bloomsbury, 1988

And the following is an influential series of essays on these novels that is in turn very revealing about *Shopping and Fucking*:

Elizabeth Young and Graham Caveney, *Shopping in Space: Essays on American 'Blank Generation' Fiction*, London, Serpent's Tail, 1992

Theatre and sexuality

Sigmund Freud, 'Character and Anal Eroticism', in *On Sexuality – Three Essays on the Theory of Sexuality and Other Works*, Harmondsworth, Penguin, 1977. [Freud's famous argument that finds a link between financial accumulation and anal eroticism would seem to have an application to *Shopping and Fucking*.]

Alan Sinfield, *Out on Stage: Lesbian and Gay Theatre in the*

Twentieth Century, New Haven and London, Yale University Press, 1999. [The best single-volume history of the representation of homosexuality on stage.]

Political background

The following, coming from a range of political perspectives are all useful in illuminating the world depicted in Ravenhill's play:

John Campbell, *Margaret Thatcher, Volume Two: The Iron Lady*, London, Pimlico, 2003

Dennis Kavanagh, *Thatcherism and British Politics: The End of Consensus?*, 2nd ed., Oxford, Oxford University Press, 1990

Naomi Klein, *No Logo: Taking Aim at the Brand Bullies*, London, Flamingo, 2000

Kenneth Minogue and Michael Biddiss (eds), *Thatcherism: Personality and Politics*, London, Macmillan, 1987

George Monbiot, *Captive State: The Corporate Takeover of Britain*, London, Macmillan, 2000

Peter Riddell, *The Thatcher Era and Its Legacy*, 2nd ed., Oxford, Blackwell, 1991

Shopping and Fucking

Shopping and Fucking was first performed at the Royal Court Theatre Upstairs, London, on 26 September 1996. The cast was as follows:

Lulu	Kate Ashfield
Robbie	Andrew Clover
Mark	James Kennedy
Gary	Antony Ryding
Brian	Robin Soans

Directed by Max Stafford-Clark
Designed by Julian McGowan
Lighting by Johanna Town
Sound by Paul Arditti

A slash in the dialogue (/) indicates that the next actor should start their line, creating overlapping speech.

Scene One

Flat – once rather stylish, now almost entirely stripped bare.

Lulu *and* **Robbie** *are trying to get* **Mark** *to eat from a carton of takeaway food.*

Lulu   Come on. Try some.

Pause.

Come on. You must eat.

Pause.

Look, please. It's delicious. Isn't that right?

Robbie   That's right.

Lulu   We've all got to eat.
Here.
Come on, come on.
A bit for me.

Mark *vomits.*

Robbie   Shit. Shit.

Lulu   Why does that alw . . . ?
Darling – could you? Let's clean this mess up.
Why does this happen?

Mark   Please.

Lulu   This will . . . come on . . . it's alright.

Mark   Look, please.

Lulu   Thank you.
See? It's going. Going . . . going . . . gone.

Robbie   Alright? OK?

Lulu   Yes, yes. He's alright now.

Mark   Look . . . you two go to bed.

Lulu   Leave you like this?

Mark   I want to be alone for a while.

Robbie   Is someone coming round?

Lulu   Do you owe money?

Mark   No. No one's coming round. Now – go to bed.

Lulu   So what are you going to do?

Mark   Just sit here. Sit and think. My head's a mess. I'm fucked.

Robbie   You'll be alright.

Mark   I'm so tired.
Look at me. I can't control anything. My . . . guts. My mind.

Robbie   We have good times don't we?

Mark   Of course we have. I'm not saying that.

Robbie   Good times. The three of us. Parties. Falling into taxis, out of taxis. Bed.

Mark   That was years ago. That was the past.

Lulu   And you said: I love you both and I want to look after you for ever.

Mark   Look I . . .

Lulu   Tell us the shopping story.

Mark   Please I want to . . .

Robbie   Yeah, come on. You still remember the shopping story.

Pause.

Mark   Well alright.
I'm watching you shopping.

Lulu   No. Start at the beginning.

Mark   That's where it starts.

Robbie   No it doesn't. It starts with: 'summer'.

Mark   Yes. OK.
It's summer. I'm in a supermarket. It's hot and I'm sweaty.
Damp. And I'm watching this couple shopping. I'm
watching you. And you're both smiling. You see me and you
know sort of straight away that I'm going to have you. You
know you don't have a choice. No control. Now this guy
comes up to me. He's a fat man. Fat and hair and lycra and
he says:
See the pair by the yoghurt?
Well, says fat guy, they're both mine. I own them. I own
them but I don't want them – because you know something?
– they're trash. Trash and I hate them. Wanna buy them?
How much?
Piece of trash like them. Let's say . . . twenty. Yeah, yours
for twenty.
So, I do the deal. I hand it over. And I fetch you. I don't
have to say anything because you know. You've seen the
transaction.
And I take you both away and I take you to my house. And
you see the house and when you see the house you know it.
You understand? You know this place.
And I've been keeping a room for you and I take you into
this room. And there's food. And it's warm. And we live out
our days fat and content and happy.

Pause.

Listen. I didn't want to say this. But I have to.
I'm going.

Lulu   Scag. Loves the scag.

Mark   Not any more.

Robbie   Loves the scag more than he loves us.

Mark   Look. Look now. That isn't fair. I hate the scag.

Lulu   Still buying the scag though, aren't you?

Mark   No. I'm off the scag. Ten days without the scag. And I'm going away.

Robbie   From us?

Mark   Yes. Tonight.

Lulu   Where are you going?

Mark   I want to get myself sorted. I need help. Someone has to sort me out.

Robbie   Don't do that. You don't need to do that. We're helping you.

Lulu   We're sorting you out.

Mark   It's not enough. I need something more.

Robbie   You're going? And leaving us?

Mark   I'm going to get help.

Robbie   Haven't we tried? We've tried. What do you think we've been doing? All this time. With the . . . clearing up when you, you . . .

Lulu   Where?

Mark   Just a place.

Lulu   Tell us.

Mark   A centre. For treatment.

Lulu   Are you coming back?

Mark   Of course I am.

Robbie   When?

Mark   Well that all depends on how well I respond. To the treatment. A few months.

Robbie   Where is it? We'll visit.

Mark   No.

Robbie   We'll come and see you.

Mark   I mustn't see you.

Robbie   I thought you loved me. You don't love me.

Mark   Don't say that. That's a silly thing to say.

Lulu   Hey. Hey, look. If you're going, then go.

Robbie   You don't love me.

Lulu   Look what you've done. Look what you've done to him.
What are you waiting for? A taxi? Maybe you want me to call a taxi? Or maybe you haven't got the money? You going to ask me for the money? Or maybe just take the money? You've sold everything. You've stolen.

Mark   Yes. It's not working. That's why I'm going.

Lulu   Yes. I think you should. No. Because we're going to be fine. We're going to do very well. And I think maybe you shouldn't come back. We won't want you back.

Mark   Let's wait and see.

Lulu   You don't own us. We exist. We're people. We can get by. Go.
Fuck right off. Go. GO.

Mark   Goodbye.

Exit **Mark**.

Robbie   Stop him. Tell him to stay. Tell him I love him.

Lulu   He's gone now. Come on. He's gone. We'll be alright. We don't need him. We'll get by.

Scene Two

Interview room.

Brian *and* **Lulu** *sit facing each other.* **Brian** *is showing* **Lulu** *an illustrated plastic plate.*

Brian   And there's this moment. This really terrific moment. Quite possibly the best moment. Because really, you see, his father is dead. Yes? The Lion King was crushed – you feel the sorrow welling up in you – crushed by a wild herd of these big cows. One moment, lord of all he surveys. And then . . . a breeze, a wind, the stamping of a hundred feet and he's gone. Only it wasn't an accident. Somebody had a plan. You see?

Lulu   Yes. I see.

Brian   Any questions. Any uncertainties. You just ask.

Lulu   Of course.

Brian   Because I want you to follow.

Lulu   Absolutely.

Brian   So then we're . . . there's . . .

Lulu   Crushed by a herd of wild cows.

Brian   Crushed by a herd of wild cows. Yes.

Lulu   Only it wasn't an accident.

Brian   Good. Excellent. Exactly. It wasn't an accident. It may have looked like an accident but. No. It was arranged by the uncle. Because –

Lulu   Because he wanted to be King all along.

Brian   Thought you said you hadn't seen it.

Lulu   I haven't.
Instinct. I have good instincts. That's one of my qualities. I'm an instinctive person.

Brian   Is that right?

Brian *writes down 'instinctive' on a pad.*

Brian   Good. Instinctive. Could be useful.

Lulu   Although of course I can also use my rational side. Where appropriate.

Brian   So you'd say you appreciate order?

Lulu   Order. Oh yes. Absolutely. Everything in its place.

Brian *writes down 'appreciates order'.*

Brian   Good. So now the father is dead. Murdered. It was the uncle. And the son has grown up. And you know – he looks like the dad. Just like him. And this sort of monkey thing comes to him. And this monkey says: 'It's time to speak to your dead dad.' So he goes to the stream and he looks in and he sees –

Lulu   / His own reflection.

Brian   his own reflection. You've never seen this?

Lulu   Never.

Brian   But then . . . The water ripples, it hazes. Until he sees a ghost. A ghost or a memory looking up at him. His . . .

Pause.

Excuse me. It takes you right here. Your throat tightens. Until . . . he sees . . . his . . . dad.
My little one. Gets to that bit and I look round and he's got these big tears in his eyes. He feels it like I do.
Because now the dad speaks. And he says: 'The time has come. It is time for you to take your place in the Cycle of Being (words to that effect). You are my son and the one true King.'
And he knows what it is he's got to do. He knows who it is he has to kill.
And that's the moment. That's our favourite bit.

Lulu   I can see that. Yes.

Brian   Would you say you in any way resembled your father?

Lulu   No. Not really. Not much.

Brian   Your mother?

Lulu   Maybe. Sometimes. Yes.

Brian   You do know who your parents are?

Lulu   Of course. We still . . . you know. Christmas. We spend Christmas together. On the whole.

Brian *writes down 'celebrates Christmas'.*

Brian   So many today are lost. Isn't that so?

Lulu   I think that's right. Yes.

Brian   And some come here. They look to me. You're looking to me, aren't you?
Well, aren't you?

Lulu   Yes. I'm looking to you.

Brian *(proffers plate)*   Here. Hold it. Just hold it up beside you. See if you look right. Smile. Look interested. Because this is special. You wouldn't want to part with this. Can you give me that look?

Lulu *attempts the look.*

Brian   That's good. Very good. Our viewers, they have to believe that what we hold up to them is special. For the right sum – life is easier, richer, more fulfilling. And you have to believe that too. Do you think you can do that?

Again **Lulu** *attempts the look.*

Brian   Good. That's very good. We don't get many in your league.

Lulu   Really?

Brian   No. That really is very . . . distinctive.

Lulu   Well. Thank you. Thanks.

Brian   And now: 'Just a few more left. So dial this number now.'

Lulu   Just a few more left. So dial this number now.

Brian   Excellent. Natural. Professional. Excellent.

Lulu   I have had training.

Brian   So you're . . . ?

Lulu   I'm a trained actress.

Brian *writes down 'trained actress'*.

Brian   I don't recognise you.

Lulu   No? Well, probably not.

Brian   Do some for me now.

Lulu   You want me to . . . ?

Brian   I want to see you doing some acting.

Lulu   I didn't realise. I haven't prepared.

Brian   Come on. You're an actress. You must be able to do some acting.
An actress – if she can't do acting when she's asked then what is she?
She's nothing.

Lulu   Alright.

She stands up.

I haven't actually done this one before. In front of anyone.

Brian   Never mind. You're doing it now.

Lulu   One day people will know what all this was for. All this suffering.

Brian   Take your jacket off.

Lulu   I'm sorry?

Brian   I'm asking you to take your jacket off. Can't act with your jacket on.

Lulu   Actually, I find it helps.

Brian   In what way?

(why so pushy?)

Lulu   The character.

Brian   Yes. But it's not helping me. I'm here to assess your talents and you're standing there acting in a jacket.

Lulu   I'd like to keep it on.

Brian (*stands*)   Alright. I'll call the girl. Or maybe you remember the way.

Lulu   No.

Brian   What do you mean – no?

Lulu   I mean . . . please I'd like this job. I want to be considered for this job.

Brian   Then we'll continue. Without the jacket. Yes?

Lulu *removes her jacket. Two chilled ready meals fall to the floor.*

Brian   Look at all this.

They both go to pick up the meals. **Brian** *gets there first.*

Exotic.

Lulu   We've got really into them. That's what we eat. For supper.

Brian   Did you pay for these?

Lulu   Yes.

Brian   Stuffed into your jacket. Did you pay for them?

Lulu   Yes.

Brian   Look me in the eyes. Did. You. Pay?

Lulu   No.

Brian   Stolen goods.

Lulu   We have to eat. We have to get by. I don't like this. I'm not a shoplifter. By nature. My instinct is for work. I need a job. Please.

Brian   You're an actress by instinct but theft is a necessity. Unless you can persuade me that I need you.
Alright. Carry on. Act a bit more.
No shirt. WTF?

Lulu   No . . .

Brian   Carry on without the . . . (what's the . . . ?) . . . blouse. And the . . .

Lulu *removes her blouse.*

Lulu   One day people will know what all this was for. All this suffering. There'll be no more mysteries. But until then we have to carry on living. We must work. That's all we can do. I'm leaving by myself tomorrow . . .

Brian (*stifling a sob*)   Oh God.

Lulu   I'm sorry. Shall I stop?

Brian   Carry on. Please.

Lulu   I'm leaving by myself tomorrow. I'll teach in a school and devote my whole life to people who need it. It's autumn now. It will soon be winter and there'll be snow everywhere. But I'll be working.
That's all.

Lulu *puts her blouse and jacket on.*

Brian (*wipes away a tear*)   Perfect. Brilliant. Did you make it up?

Lulu   No. I learnt it. From a book.

Brian   Brilliant. So you think you can sell?

Lulu   I know I can sell.

Brian   Because you're an actress?

Lulu   It helps.

Brian   You seem very confident.

Lulu   I am.

Brian   Alright then. A trial. Something by way of a test. I'm going to give you something to sell and we're going to see how well you do. Clear so far?

Lulu   Totally.

Brian   You understand that I am *entrusting* you?

Lulu   I understand.

Brian   I am entrusting you to pass this important test.

Lulu   I'm not going to let you down.

Brian *reaches for his briefcase and starts to open it.*

[handwritten margin note: What is actually happening]

Scene Three

Flat.

Robbie *is sitting. He is wearing the uniform of a leading burger chain.* **Lulu** *stands over him.*

Robbie   And all I've said was: With cheese, sir?
And he just looks at me blankly. Just stares into my eyes.
And there's this . . . fear.
Try again. 'Would you like cheese on your burger, sir?'
This is too much for him. I see the bottom lip go. The eyes are filling up.

Lulu   So you told him. And they sacked you?

Robbie   Someone had to. If you were there you'd . . . I decided I'm going to have to tell him. And I say: Look, here you have a choice. For once in your life you have a choice so for fuck's sake make the most of it.

Lulu   And then they / sacked you?

Robbie   And then. He gets his fork. Grabs this fork. And he jumps over the counter. And he goes for me.

Lulu   With the fork?

Robbie   Goes for me with the fork. Gets me down and stabs me.

Lulu   He stabbed you?

Beat.

Robbie   It's nothing.

Lulu   You're wounded. You should have told me.

Robbie   No. It's nothing.

Lulu   Where's the wound then?

Robbie   It snapped. Before it did any damage.

Lulu   ?

Robbie   The fork. It was a plastic fork. It snapped before it did any damage.

Pause.

Lulu   So . . . no wound? So. Where's the money going to come from? Who's gonna pay for everything?

Robbie   You'll come up with something.

Lulu   Me?

Robbie   Yeah. You'll sort it out.
Did you get it?

Lulu   Did I get . . . ?

Robbie   The job. The TV.

Lulu   Well. Yes. They're taking me on . . .

Robbie   Brilliant/ That's brilliant.

Lulu   They're offering me a sort of temporary assignment.

Robbie   Yeah? What sort of . . . ?

Lulu *produces three hundred E in a clear plastic bag.*

Robbie   You're gonna sell them?

Lulu   We're going to sell them. You can make yourself useful.
Should be three hundred. You can count them.

Exit **Lulu**. **Robbie** *starts counting the tablets.* **Mark** *enters and watches* **Robbie**, *who doesn't see him until* –

Mark   Are you dealing?

Robbie   Fuck. You made me –
How long have you – ?

Mark   Just now. Are you dealing?

Robbie   That doesn't . . .

Pause.

So. They let you out.

Mark   Sort of.

Pause.

Robbie   Thought you said months. Did you miss me?

Mark   I missed you both.

Robbie   I missed you. So. I s'pose . . .
I sort of hoped you'd miss me.

Mark   Yeah. Right.

Robbie *moves to* **Mark**. *They kiss.*

Robbie *moves to kiss* **Mark** *again.*

Mark   No.

Robbie   No?

Mark   Sorry.

Robbie   No. That's OK.

Mark   No, sorry. I mean it. Because actually I'd decided I wasn't going to do that. I didn't really want that to happen, you know? Commit myself so quickly to . . . intimacy.

Robbie   OK.

Mark   Just something I'm trying to work through.

Robbie   . . . Work through?

Mark   Yeah. Sort out. In my head.
We've been talking a lot about dependencies. Things you get dependent on.

Robbie   Smack.

Mark   Smack, yes absolutely. But also people. You get dependent on people. Like . . . emotional dependencies. Which are just as addictive, OK?

Robbie (*pause*)   So – that's it, is it?

Mark   No.

Robbie   That's me finished.

Mark   No.

Robbie   'Goodbye.'

Mark   I didn't say that. No. Not goodbye.

Robbie   Then . . . kiss me.

Mark   Look . . . (*Turns away.*)

Robbie   Fuck off.

Mark   Until I've worked this through.

Pause.

Robbie   Did you use?

Mark   No.

Robbie   Right. You used, they chucked you out.

Mark   Nothing. I'm clean.

Robbie   So . . .

Pause.

Mark   There are these rules, you see. They make you sign
– you agree to this set of rules. One of which I broke.
OK?

Robbie   Which one?

Mark   It was nothing.

Robbie   Come on.

Mark   I told them. It wasn't like that. I put my case /
but –

Robbie   *Tell me.*

Pause.

Mark   No personal relations.

Robbie   Fuck.

Mark   You're not supposed to – form an attachment.

Robbie   Ah, I see.

Mark   Which I didn't.

Robbie   So that's why / you won't kiss me.

Mark   It wasn't an attachment.

Robbie (*pause*)   If you were just honest. / We said we'd be
honest.

Mark   It wasn't like that. I told them 'You can't call this a
personal relationship.'

Robbie   What was it then?

Mark   More of a . . . transaction. I paid him. I gave him
money. And when you're paying, you can't call that a
personal relationship, can you? / What would you call it?

Robbie   You can't kiss me. You fucked someone but you can't kiss me.

Mark   That would mean something.

Robbie   Who was it?

Mark   Somebody.

Robbie   Tell me who.

Mark   He was called Wayne.

Robbie   Well get you.

Mark   I just – you know – in the shower. Shower and I . . . Saw his bottom. Saw the hole, you know. And I felt like – I wanted to . . . lick it.

Robbie (*pause*)   That's it?

Mark   We did a deal. I paid him. We confined ourselves to the lavatory. It didn't mean anything.

Robbie   Nothing for afters?

Mark   That's all.

Robbie   Just Lick and Go.

Mark   It wasn't a personal relation.

Robbie (*lets trousers drop*)   Well, if you can't kiss my mouth.

Mark   No. With you – there's . . . baggage.

Robbie   Well, excuse me. I'll just have to grow out of it.

Robbie *pulls his trousers up. Pause.*

Mark   I'm sorry.

Robbie   Sorry? No. It's not . . . sorry doesn't work. Sorry's not good enough.

Pause.

Mark   You're dealing?

Robbie   Doesn't matter.

Mark   Thought so.

Robbie   Listen, this stuff is happiness. Little moment of heaven. And if I'm spreading a little – no a great big fuck off load of happiness –

Pause. **Robbie** *picks up an E between thumb and forefinger.*

Mark   It's not real.

Robbie   Listen, if you, if this, this . . . planet is real . . .

He takes an E. Pause.

Waiting for you. Do you know what it's like – waiting? Looking forward to this day – for you to . . . And you – Oh fuck it. Fuck it all.

Robbie *takes another E.*

Enter **Lulu** *with two microwaved ready meals on a tray.*

Lulu   I . . . They let you out. It's sooner . . .

Mark   Yeah. They let me out. Thought I'd come back. See if you're alright.

Pause.

Lulu   I've only got enough for two.

Mark   Never mind.

Lulu   It's just hard to share them. They're done individually.

Mark   Oh well.

Lulu   Well . . . hello.

Mark   Hello.

Lulu   We've got really into the little boxes with the whole thing in it. One each.

Robbie   Looks great, doesn't she?
Gonna be on TV, aren't you?

Lulu   They're . . . considering it. It's just a / little . . .

Robbie   Just she says. Only. It's TV.

Mark   Great.

Robbie   You see, we're doing something? Aren't we?

Lulu   Yes.

Robbie   We're working. Providing.

Mark   So will I. Yes. I'll sort myself out and we'll be OK.

Lulu   They're really not made for sharing. It's difficult.

Mark   It's OK. I'll go out.

Robbie   Back to Wayne?

Mark   No. Out. Find some food. Shopping.

Robbie   Don't just – don't stand there and judge us.

Mark   Cheeseburger. Some chocolate maybe.

Robbie   I want you to be part of this.

Mark   I've hurt you. I see that. But – please just let me . . .
I've got to take this a step at a time, OK?

Exit **Mark**.

Robbie   Cunt. Cunt. / Cunt.

Lulu   I know, I know.

Robbie   Hate the cunt.

Lulu   That's it. Come on. / Come on.

Robbie   Hate him now.

Lulu   Yes. Yes. Yes.

Robbie   I want him to suffer.

Pause.

Lulu   Did you count them?

Robbie   Oh. Yes. Yesyesyes.

Lulu   And was it? Three hundred. Exactly.

Robbie   Yes. Three hundred. Exactly.

Scene Four

A bedsit.

Gary *is sitting on a tatty armchair.* **Mark** *is standing.*

Gary   Course, any day now it'll be virtual. That's what they reckon.

Mark   I suppose that's right.

Gary   I'm planning on that. Looking to invest. The Net and the Web and that. You ever done that?

Mark   No. Never.

Gary   Couple of years' time and we'll not even meet. We'll be like holograph things. We could look like whatever we wanted. And then we wouldn't want to meet 'cos we might not look like our holographs. You know what I mean? I think a lot about that kind of stuff me.
See, I called you back. Don't do that for everyone.

Mark   Thank you.

Gary   Why d'ya pick me?

Mark   I liked your voice.

Gary   There must have been something special.

Mark   I just thought you had a nice voice.

Gary   How old did you think I was – on the lines?

Mark   I didn't think about it.

Gary   How old do you want me to be?

Mark   It doesn't matter.

Gary   Everybody's got an age they want you to be.

Mark   I'd like you to be yourself.

Gary   That's a new one.

Mark   I'd like to keep things straightforward.

Gary   You're in charge. Make yerself at home.
D'you want porn? I mean, it's mostly women and that but it's something.
(*Indicating porn.*) She looks rough, doesn't she? Would you shag her?

Mark   No. Let's leave the porn.

Gary   Or we could do some like . . . stuff, y'know.

He pulls out a packet of cocaine.

Share it with you.

Mark   No. Thank you.

Gary   It's thrown in. There's no extra cost.

Mark   I don't want any.

Gary   It's quality. He don't give me rubbish.

Mark   Put it away.

Gary   I int gonna poison ya.

Mark   Put the fucking stuff away.

Gary   Alright, alright. Don't get knocky.

Pause.

Mark   I'm going to have to go.

Gary   You only just got here.

Mark   I can't be around people who use.

Gary   Alright. Look. I'm putting it away.

He puts the packet in his trouser pocket.

See? All gone.
You stopping?

Mark   I'm sorry. I'm really sorry but I suppose I was
threatened by your actions. And my fear led me to an . . .
outburst. Which I now regret. It's just very important to me.
And I'd like you to acknowledge that.

Gary   You God Squad?

Mark   I'm sorry?

Gary   I had 'em before. We're at it and he kept going on
about Lamb of Jesus. Hit me. I give as good as I took.

Mark   No. I'm not God Squad.

Gary   Just got a thing about druggies?

Mark   I have a history of substance abuse.

Gary   You're a druggie?

Mark   I'm a recovering substance abuser.

Gary   You're not a druggie?

Mark   I used to be a druggie.

Gary   Got you. So what you into?

Mark   You mean . . .

Gary   Sexwise.

Mark   Sexwise, I'd say I'm into the usual things.

Gary   So, you're looking for regular?

Mark   Pretty regular. The important thing for me right
now, for my needs, is that this doesn't actually mean
anything, you know?
Which is why I wanted something that was a transaction.

Because I thought if I pay then it won't mean anything. Do you think that's right – in your experience?

Gary   Reckon.

Mark   Because this is a very important day for me. I'm sorry, I'm making you listen.

Gary   Everyone wants you to listen.

Mark   Right. Well. Today you see is my first day of a new life. I've been away to get better, well to acknowledge my needs anyway, and now I'm starting again and I suppose I wanted to experiment with you in terms of an interaction that was sexual but not personal, or at least not needy, OK?

A distant sound of coins clattering.

Gary   Downstairs. The arcade. Somebody's just had a win. You gotta know which ones to play otherwise all you get is tokens. I've a lucky streak me. Good sound, int it? Chinkchinkchinkchinkchink.

Mark   I suppose what I'd like, what I'd really like is to lick your arse.

Gary   That all?

Mark   Yes. That's all.

Gary   Right. We can settle up now.

Mark   How much do you want?

Gary   Hundred.

Mark   A hundred pounds? No, I'm sorry.

Gary   Alright. If it's just licking, fifty.

Mark   Look, I can give you twenty.

Gary   Twenty. What d'you expect for twenty?

Mark   It's all I've got.
I've got to keep ten for the taxi.

Gary   You're taking the piss, int ya?

Mark   Look, I'll walk. Thirty. It's all I've got.

Gary   I should kick you out, you know that? I shouldn't be wasting my time with losers like you. Look at you. Druggie with thirty quid. I'm in demand me. I don't have to be doing this.
There's a bloke, right, rich bloke, big house. Wants me to live with him.
So tell me: why should I let you lick my arse?

Mark   Why don't you think of him? You could lie there and think of him.
Just a few minutes, OK? Thirty quid.
Just get my tongue up, wiggle it about and you can think of him.
This isn't a personal thing. It's a transaction, OK?

Gary *pulls down his trousers and underpants.* **Mark** *starts to lick* **Gary***'s arse.*

Gary   He's a big bloke. Cruel like but really really he's kind. Phones me on the lines and says: 'I really like the sound of you. I want to look after you.'

Clatter of coins.

Listen to that. They're all winning tonight.
So I'll probably move in. Yeah, probably do it tomorrow.

Mark *pulls away. There's blood around his mouth.*

Mark   There's blood.

Pause.

You're bleeding.

Gary   Didn't think that happened any more.
Thought I'd healed, OK? That's not supposed to happen.
I'm not infected, OK?
Punter gave me a bottle somewhere. Rinse it out.

Mark *goes to take the money.*

Gary   You can't take that.
Lick me arse you said. Licked me arse didn't ya?

Mark   I'll leave you ten.

Gary   Rinse your mouth out.
We agreed thirty.

Mark   Twenty. I need ten for the taxi.

Gary   Thirty – look, I need the money – please – I owe
him downstairs – can't live on tokens – give me the thirty.
You promised.

Mark   Have the thirty.

Mark *gives* **Gary** *the thirty pounds.*

Gary   Stay. Rinse it out. You'll feel better. It's
champagne.

Gary *exits.* **Mark** *sits.*

Scene Five

Pub.

Robbie *hands* **Lulu** *a drink.*

Robbie   After ten minutes I thought I'd got the wrong
name. Checked the name. And then I thought: maybe it's
the right name but the wrong pub. Because there could be
two pubs with the same name. But probably not on the
same street. So I checked. And there wasn't. The same
name on this street. But then I thought there could be other
streets with the same street name. So I looked it up,
borrowed the book from this bloke and looked it – listen.
Did you know? There's blood.

Lulu   On me?

Robbie   On you. You've got blood on your face.

Lulu   I thought so. Get it off.

Robbie   Why's that then?

Lulu   Please I want it off.

Robbie   Is that your blood?

Lulu (*pawing at her face*)   Where is it?

Robbie (*indicates forehead*)   Just – yeah – that's it.

Lulu   Is it all gone? Everything?

Robbie   Yes. It's all gone.
Was that your blood?

Lulu   No. It must have splashed me.

Robbie   Whose blood is it?

Lulu   Why does it have to be like this?

Robbie   I knew something was up.

Lulu   I mean, what kind of planet is this when you can't
even buy a bar of chocolate?

Robbie   I think that's why I worried so much.

Lulu   And afterwards of course you feel so guilty. Like you
could have done something.

Robbie   They attacked you?

Lulu   Not me. The Seven-Eleven.
Walking past and I think: I'd like a bar of chocolate. So I go
in but I can't decide which one. There's so much choice.
Too much. Which I think they do deliberately. I'm only
partly aware – and really why should I be any more aware?
– that an argument is forming at the counter. A bloke.
Dirty, pissy sort of –

Robbie   Wino?

Lulu   Probably. Wino sort of bloke is having a go at this
girl, young –

Robbie   Student?

Lulu   Yes. Student girl behind the counter. Wino is raising his voice to student.
There's a couple of us in there. Me – chocolate. Somebody else – TV guides. (Because now of course they've made the choice on TV guides so fucking difficult as well.)
And wino's shouting: You've given me twenty. I asked for a packet of ten and you've given me twenty.
And I didn't see anything. Like the blade or anything. But I suppose he must have hit her artery. Because there was blood everywhere.

Robbie   Shit.

Lulu   And he's stabbing away and me and TV guide we both just walked out of there and carried on walking.
And I can't help thinking: why did we do that?

Robbie   Look. It's done now.

Lulu   I could have stayed.
Am I clean?

Robbie   All gone.

Lulu   I could have intervened. Stopped him.
It's all off?

Robbie   Yes.

Lulu   It's like it's not really happening there – the same time, the same place as you. You're here. And it's there.
And you just watch.
I'm going back.

Robbie   What for?

Lulu   Who called an ambulance? She could be lying there.

Robbie   No. There must have been someone.

Lulu   Or I could give a description.

Robbie   Did you see his face?

Lulu   No. No, I didn't.

Robbie   He's a wino. How they going to find a wino out there?

Lulu   I don't know.

Robbie   Look, they'll have a video. There's always like a security camera. They'll have his face.

Lulu   And I've still got. You see I took.

She produces the chocolate bar from her pocket.

I took the bar of chocolate. She's being attacked and I picked this up and just for a moment I thought: I can take this and there's nobody to stop me. Why did I do that? What am I?

Pause.

Robbie   They must be used to it. Work nights in a shop like that, what do they expect?
You go home.

Lulu   I can't.

Robbie   You've had a shock. You need to rest.

Lulu   We've got to do this.

Robbie   I know.

Lulu   We've got to do it tonight.

Robbie   You're in no fit state. You've gotta sleep.

Lulu   I don't want to sleep. I want to get on with this.

Robbie   I'll do it.

Lulu   We've got to do it together.

Robbie   Think I can't manage? I can cope.

Lulu   Of course you can.

Robbie   I want to do it.

Lulu   Out there on your own?

Robbie   I'm educated. I've read the books. I've got the bits of paper. It's only selling. I can sell. Go home. Go to bed.

Lulu   You're right. I am tired.

Robbie   Then sleep.

Lulu   They'll have me on the video. With the chocolate.

Robbie   They'll be after him. Not you.

Lulu   Suppose.
It's all here.

Lulu *gives* **Robbie** *a bum-bag.*

Robbie   Right then.

Lulu   Look there's just one rule, OK? That's what they reckon. If you're dealing. There's just rule number one. Which is: He who sells shall not use.

Robbie   Yeah. Makes sense, doesn't it?

Lulu   Right. So just don't . . .

Robbie   Course not. Rule number one. I'm a big boy.

Lulu (*hands* **Robbie** *flyer*)   Show them this on the door.

Robbie   Still love you.

Lulu   Haven't said that for a long time. Wish we could go back to before. Just you and me.
Do you think I look great?

Robbie   In the right light. And a fair wind.

Lulu   And a couple of E?

Robbie   . . . I better go.

Exit **Robbie**.

Lulu *looks at the chocolate bar for a beat. Then eats it very quickly.*

Scene Six

Bedsit.

Gary *hands* **Mark** *the bottle of champagne.*

Gary   Horrible int it? Little kid with his arse bleeding.

Mark   Sorry. I need to go.

Gary   Arse like a sore.

Mark   It's not that.

Gary   Thought I'd healed.

Mark   Yes, yes. Sure.

Gary   This bloke, my mum's bloke . . .

Mark   No. Don't, please.

Gary   I tried to fight him off, but I think he gets off on that.

Mark   Please, if you . . .

Gary   Whatever, you lie back, you fight, he still . . . I started to bleed.

Mark   No.

Gary   He comes into my room after *News at Ten* . . . every night after *News at Ten* and it's, son. Come here, son. I fucking hate that, 'cos I'm not his son.

Mark   Sure, sure. I understand.

Gary   But I thought . . . now . . . I . . . got . . . away.

Mark   FUCKING SHUT UP OK? KEEP YOUR FUCKING MOUTH SHUT.

Gary   Sound like him.

Mark   Listen. I want you to understand because. I have this personality you see? Part of me that gets addicted. I have a tendency to define myself purely in terms of my

relationship to others. I have no definition of myself you see.
So I attach myself to others as a means of avoidance, of
avoiding knowing the self. Which is actually potentially very
destructive. For me – destructive for me. I don't know if
you're following this but you see if I don't stop myself I
repeat the patterns. Get attached to people to these
emotions then I'm back to where I started. Which is why,
though it may seem uncaring, I'm going to have to go.
You're gonna be OK?
I'm sorry it's just –

Gary *cries.*

Mark   Hey. Hey. Hey.

*He makes a decision. He takes **Gary** in his arms.*

Come on. No. Come on. Please. It's OK.
Everything will be OK.
You don't have to say anything.

Gary   I want a dad. I want to be watched. All the time,
someone watching me. Do you understand?

Mark   I think so.

Gary   Does everyone feel like that?

Mark   Well . . . no.

Gary   What do you want?

Mark   I don't know yet.

Gary   You must want something. Everybody's got
something.

Mark   I used to know what I felt. I traded. I made money.
Tic Tac. And when I made money I was happy, when I lost
money I was unhappy. Then things got complicated. But for
so many years everything I've felt has been . . . chemically
induced. I mean, everything you feel you wonder . . . maybe
it's just the . . .

Gary   The smack.

Mark   Yes. The smack, coffee, you know, or the fags.

Gary   The microwaves.

Mark   The cathode rays.

Gary   The madcow. Moooooo.

Mark   Right. I mean, are there any feelings left, you know?

The coins clatter.

I want to find out, want to know if there are any feelings left.

Gary (*offering two Pot Noodles*)   Beef or Nice and Spicy?

Scene Seven

Accident and Emergency waiting room.

Robbie *sits bruised and bleeding.* **Lulu** *is holding a bottle of TCP.*

Lulu   I asked the Sister. She said I could. It'll sting a bit. But with blood. It might get infected. Like gangrene.

Lulu *applies the TCP to* **Robbie***'s face.*

Lulu   Keep still. Don't want to end up with like – one eye mmm?
Look good actually.

Robbie   Yeah.

Lulu   Yes, suits you. Makes you look – well . . . tough.

Robbie   Good.

Lulu   I could go for you. Some people a bruise, a wound, doesn't suit them.

Robbie   No.

Lulu   But you – it fits. It belongs.

Lulu *slips her hand into* **Robbie**'*s trousers and starts to play with his genitals.*

Lulu   Is that good?

Robbie   Yeah.

Lulu   That's it. Come on. That's it.
Tell me about them.

Robbie   Who?

Lulu   The men. Attackers.

Robbie   Them.

Lulu   The attackers. Muggers.

Robbie   Well.

Lulu   Sort of describe what they did. Like a story.

Robbie   No.

Lulu   I want to know.

Robbie   It's nothing.

Lulu   I don't want to just imagine.

Robbie   It wasn't like that.

Lulu   Come on then.

Robbie   Look.

Lulu   What was it like?

Pause.

Robbie   There was only one.

Lulu   Didn't you say gang?

Robbie   No.
Just this one bloke.

Lulu   A knife?

Robbie   No.

Lulu   Oh.
So. He pinned you down?

Robbie   No.

Lulu   Got the money.

Robbie   I didn't – there wasn't any money alright? I
never took any money.

Lulu   You never / sold?

Robbie   No.

Lulu   So before you even got there this man. With his
knife –

Robbie   / There wasn't a knife.

Lulu   Attacks and gets the E.

Robbie   No. I got there. I was there with the E.

Lulu   So?

Robbie   So.

Pause.

Lulu   You've lost it. (*His erection.*)

Robbie   Yeah.

Lulu   Gone limp on me.

Robbie   Yeah.

Lulu   Why's that then?

Pause.

Robbie   I was there. I was all ready. I was ready to deal.

Lulu   Right.

Robbie   There's a few other dealers. Stood around the
dance floor. I take up my position. I'm ready.
And this bloke comes up to me. Really, really nice-looking.

And he says: 'You selling?' Yeah, I say. Fifteen quid a go.
And the way he looks at me I know he fancies me, you
know?
And he reaches in his pocket and – oh shit. So stupid.

Lulu   It was the knife yes?

Robbie   There wasn't a knife.

Lulu   Gun?

Robbie   He. Look. He reaches in his pocket and says:
'Shit I left my money in my other jeans. Oh shit, now how
am I gonna have a good time, now how am I gonna enjoy
myself?'

Lulu   Right. Yes.
Go on.

Robbie   And he looked so . . . I felt sorry for him, alright?
But then he says: 'How about this? How about you give me
the E? Give me the E now then later, at the end, you can
come back to mine and we can get the money from my
jeans.'

Lulu   Right so he was luring you. Luring you back to his /
place.

Robbie   No.

Lulu   Get you back to his so that he could pull the gun /
or whatever.

Robbie   No.

Lulu   And get the Es off you.

Robbie   No, it didn't happen. That's not it.

Lulu   No?

Robbie   No.
So I said yes. It's a deal. And I gave him the E and he takes
it and I watch him and he's dancing and he's sweating and

smiling and he looks – well – beautiful and just really really happy.

Lulu   How many?

Robbie   What?

Lulu   You broke the first rule – yes? Yes?

Robbie   Yes.

Lulu   How many?

Robbie   I was out there on my own.

Lulu   How many?

Robbie   Three. Maybe four.

Lulu   Shit. I told you. Rule number one.

Robbie   I know.
But then, a few minutes later. A bloke. Even better, yes, even better looking than the last bloke. And he says: 'Look, you gave my mate some E and I was wondering, I get paid at the end of the week and if I give you my phone number will you give me a couple of E?'

Lulu   You didn't?

Robbie   Yes.

Lulu   Fuck.

Robbie   And I felt good, I felt amazing, from just giving, you see?

Lulu   No, no I don't.

Robbie   But imagine. Imagine you're there, imagine how it feels.

Lulu   No.

Robbie   And then – it sort of rolled. It flew.

Lulu   You prick. Three hundred.

Robbie   Until there's these guys, they're asking and I'm giving and everyone's dancing and smiling.

Lulu   Three hundred E. / Silly prick.

Robbie   Listen, listen to me. This is what I felt.

Lulu   I don't want to know. / You gave away three hundred.

Robbie   It's important.

Lulu   No. Stupid. Fucking. / Cunt.

Robbie   Just listen for a moment, OK?
Listen, this is the important bit. If you'd felt . . . I felt.
I was looking down on this planet. Spaceman over this earth. And I see this kid in Rwanda, crying, but he doesn't know why. And this granny in Kiev, selling everything she's ever owned. And this president in Bogota or . . . South America. And I see the suffering. And the wars. And the grab, grab, grab.
And I think: Fuck Money. Fuck it. This selling. This buying. This system. Fuck the bitching world and let's be . . . beautiful. Beautiful. And happy. You see?
You see?
But now you see, but then I've only got two left and this bloke comes up and says: 'You the bloke giving out the E?' I give him the two but he says 'What two? Two. Two's not going to do shit for me. You gotta have more.' And he starts to hit, he starts to punch me.

Lulu   Fucking fucker arsehole. Fuck.
Pillowbiter. (*Hit*.) Shitstabber. (*Hit*.)
Boys grow up you know and stop playing with each other's willies. Men and women make the future. There are people out there who need me. Normal people who have kind tidy sex and when they want it. And boys? Boys just fuck each other.
The suffering is going to be handed out. And I shouldn't be part of that. But it'll be both of us. And that's not justice. Is it?

You look like shit now. Look like you might get (*Throws the bottle of TCP into* **Robbie**'s *eyes*.) gangrene.

Exit **Lulu**.

Robbie   Nurse. Nurse.

Scene Eight

Bedsit.

Mark *and* **Gary**.

Gary   I knew it wasn't right. I went to the council.
And I said to her, look, it's simple: he's fucking me.
Once, twice, three times a week he comes into my room.
He's a big man. He holds me down and he fucks me. How long? she says. About two years, I say. I say he moved in then six months later it starts. I told her and she says 'Does he use a condom?' ·

Mark   Yeah?

Gary   Yeah. I mean 'Does he use a condom?'
When it's like that he's not gonna use a condom, is he? Just spit. All he used is a bit of spit.

Mark   On his – ?

Gary   Spit on his dick.

Mark   Of course.

Gary   And then she / says –

Mark   / And you –

Gary   The next thing / she says –

Mark   Does he / spit –

Gary   I told her that and / she says –

Mark   Does he spit up you?

Gary   Listen. I tell her he's fucking me – without a condom – and she says to me – you know what she says?

Mark   No. No, I don't.

Gary   I think I've got a leaflet. Would you like to give him a leaflet?

Mark   Fuck.

Gary   Yeah. Give him a leaflet.

Mark   Well –

Gary   No, I don't want a leaflet. I mean, what good is a fucking leaflet? He can't even read a fucking leaflet, you know.

Mark   Yes.

Gary   And there's this look – like . . . panic in her eyes and she says: What do you want me to do?

Mark   Right.

Gary   Tell me what you want me to do.

Mark   And you said.

Gary   Well, I don't know. Inject him with something, put him away, cut something off. Do something. And I'm – I've got this anger, right? This great big fucking anger – here in front of my eyes. I mean, I fucking hate her now, right?

Mark   So did you / attack?

Gary   I go: Fuck. Fuck.

Mark   Maybe a knife or something?

Gary   So. In this little box, little white box room . . .

Mark   You attacked / her?

Gary   I stand on the table and I shout:
It's not difficult this is it? It's easy this. He's my stepdad. Listen, he's my stepdad and he's fucking me.

And I walk away and I get on the coach and I come down here and I'm never going back. Gonna find something else. Because there's this bloke. Looking out for me. He'll come and collect me. Take me to this big house/

Mark   Look, this person that you're looking for . . .

Gary   Yeah?

Mark   Well it's not me.

Gary   Of course not.

Mark   No.

Gary   Fuck, you didn't think . . . ? No. It's not meant to be you. You and me we're looking for different things, right?

Mark   Right.

Gary   Mates?

Mark   Mates.

Gary   So – mate – do you wanna stay?

Mark   I don't know.

Gary   Stay if you like. Room on the floor. Someone waiting up for you?

Mark   Not exactly.

Gary   You stay long as you want.

Mark   Thank you.

Gary   Stay around and you can keep yourself busy. Give us a hand. Getting the messages, cleaning up. Chucking out the mental ones.
Tell you what, you hang around long enough we can . . .

He pulls out a holdall from behind the chair.
He unzips the bag. It is full of fifty-pence pieces. He catches up handfuls and lets them cascade through his fingers.

See? I'm a winner me. Every time. And I don't let them give
me tokens.
I can pay for what I want.
Stick around, you and me could go shopping yeah?

Mark   I don't know.

Gary   It's only shopping.

Mark   Alright then. Yeah. Let's go shopping.

They both listen to the coins as they run through **Gary**'s *fingers.*

Scene Nine

Flat.

Brian, **Lulu** *and* **Robbie**. **Brian** *inserts a video.*

Brian   Watch. I want you to see this.

*They watch a video of a schoolboy playing a cello. They sit for some
time in silence.* **Brian** *starts to weep.*

Sorry. Sorry.

Lulu   Would you like a – something to wipe?

Brian   Silly. Me a grown man.

Lulu   Maybe a handkerchief?

Brian   No. No.

*He pulls himself together. They sit and watch again for some time, but
eventually he starts to weep again.*

Oh God. I'm so – I'm really sorry.

Lulu   No, no.

Brian   It's just the beauty, you see? The beauty of it.

Lulu   Of course.

Brian   Like a memory, you know, memory of what we've lost.

Pause.

Lulu   Are you sure you don't want – ?

Brian   Well –

Lulu   It's no problem.

Brian   Well then.

Lulu (*to* **Robbie**)   Could you – ?

Robbie   No problem.

Robbie *exits. They continue to watch the video.* **Robbie** *enters again with a toilet roll, takes it over to* **Brian**.

Brian   What's this?

Robbie   It's for your – you know to wipe your –

Brian   I asked you what it is.

Robbie   Well.

Brian   So tell me what it is. What is in your hand?

Robbie   Well –

Lulu   Darling.

Brian   Yes?

Robbie   Toilet paper.

Brian   Toilet paper exactly. Toilet paper. Which belongs in the –

Robbie   Toilet.

Brian   Exactly.

Lulu   Darling, I didn't mean . . . that.

Brian   And we use it to – ?

Robbie   Well, wipe your arse.

Brian   Exactly. Wipe your arse. While I – what is this?
(*Wipes eye.*)

Lulu   I didn't mean toilet paper.

Robbie   It's a – like a tear.

Brian   It is a tear. Little drop of pure emotion. Which
requires a – ?

Robbie   Well, a hanky.

Brian   Handkerchief.

Robbie   Handkerchief.

Lulu   Of course, I meant a handkerchief.

Brian   This is disrupting you know that?

Lulu   Sorry.

Brian   This isn't – we're not in a supermarket or, or a
disco. Music like this, you listen.

Lulu   Yes.

Again they all settle down to watch the video. After a while, **Brian**
starts to cry, but even more so this time.

Brian   Oh God. Oh God. God.

Lulu   He's very good.

Brian   You feel it like – like something you knew.
Something so beautiful that you've lost but you'd forgotten
that you've lost it. Then you hear this.

Lulu   Play like that when he's how . . . how old?

Brian   Hear this and knew what you've . . . l-l-l-ooost.

Brian *starts to sob heavily.*

Lulu   Look, I think I've got one.

Robbie   A handkerchief?

Lulu   Yes. A handkerchief. In the bedroom.

Robbie   Shall I fetch it?

Lulu   Well – yes. Yes, I think you should.

Exit **Robbie**.

Brian   Because once it was paradise, you see? And you could hear it – heaven singing in your eyes. But we sinned, and God took it away, took away music until we forgot we even heard it but sometimes you get a sort of glimpse – music or a poem – and it reminds you of what it was like before all the sin.

Enter **Robbie**, *offers handkerchief to* **Brian**.

Brian   Is it clean?

Robbie   Yes.

Brian   Again – is it clean?

Robbie   Yes.

Brian   Again – is it clean?

Robbie   Yes.

Brian   Look me in the eyes. Straight in the eyes. Yes?

Robbie (*does so*)   Yes.

Brian   And again – is it clean?

Robbie   No.

Brian   Then why did you offer it to me?

Robbie   Well –

Brian   Dirty handkerchief. Offer a dirty handkerchief.

Lulu   Darling –

Brian   Handkerchief for your nose.

Brian *punches* **Robbie**. *He slumps to the floor.*

Robbie   I'm – sorry.

Lulu   Take it away.

Robbie   Yes. Sorry.

Robbie *crawls out as they settle down in front of the video.*

Brian   His teacher says – and it's a religious school, very
religious school – his teacher says 'It's a gift from God.' And
I think that's right. Think that must be right because it can't
be from us. Doesn't come from me and his mother. I mean,
where does it come from if it's not from God, eh? Kid like
that, nice kid – his father's son – but nothing special, picks
up a bit of wood and string and – well – grown men cry.

Lulu   You must be very proud.

Robbie *enters.* **Brian** *removes a pristine handkerchief from his top
pocket and carefully wipes his eyes.*

Brian (*to* **Robbie**)   See. You don't wipe your eyes with
something that's been up your nose, alright?

Robbie   Yes. Sorry.

They continue to watch the video.

Brian   Think of the life he's gonna have, eh? Think of
that.

Pause.

Because he doesn't know it now of course. But when he's
older, when he knows about sin, about all this, then he's
gonna thank God he's got this, isn't he? This little bit of
purity.

Lulu   It is amazing, isn't it?

Robbie   Yeah. Yeah. Really – amazing.

Lulu   That it just looks so effortless.

Brian   But there is effort.

Lulu   Of course.

Brian   Behind it all is effort.

Lulu   Have to practise all the time, don't they?

Brian   His effort – yes.

Lulu   For like – hours a day.

Brian   His efforts – of course – but also my efforts.

Lulu   Of course.

Brian   Because, at the end of the day, at the final reckoning, behind beauty, behind God, behind paradise, peel them away and what is there? (*To* **Robbie**.) Son, I'm asking you.

Robbie   Well –

Brian   Come on, son.

Robbie   Well –

Brian   Answer the question.

Robbie   Well – a father.

Brian   Sorry?

Robbie   You can't have them without a sort of a dad.

Brian   No. No. Think again. Try again.

Robbie   Well I –

Brian   Think.

Robbie   No.

Brian   No, no. That's not good enough – no. Behind beauty, behind God, behind paradise –

Lulu   Darling . . . ?

Robbie   Money.

Brian   Yes. Good. Excellent. Money. Takes a few knocks, doesn't it, son?
Yeah.

But we get it knocked into us don't we, eh? Learn the rules. Money. There's boarding fees and the uniforms, the gear, the music, skiing.
Which is why I run such a tight ship you see? Which is why I have to keep the cash flow flowing you see? Which is why I can't let people FUCK. ME. AROUND. You understand?

Lulu   Of course.

Brian   Which is why, right now, I feel sad and sort of angry. Yes?

Lulu   Yes.

Brian   I don't like mistakes. I don't like my mistakes. And now you tell me I've made a mistake. And so I hate myself. Inside. My soul.
We have a problem. Three thousand pounds of a problem. But what is the solution?

They sit for a moment and contemplate this. Finally, **Brian** *gets up, ejects the video, puts it back into its case.*

This could be a stalemate. Unless one of us concedes. But would you concede? Could you concede anything?

Lulu   No.

Brian   So what you're saying is – you're asking me to concede.

Lulu   Yes.

Brian   You think I should concede?

Long pause.

Seven days. To make the money.

Lulu   Thank you.

Brian   You understand? Son?

Robbie   Yes. Seven days. Yes.

Pause. **Brian** *produces a second video.*

Brian   I'd like you to have a look at this. Camera's a bit shaky. Some people will tell you it's about 'production values'. But really . . . 'production values'? They're nothing without a good subject.
This one was recorded a couple of months ago. 11.53am. On a Wednesday.

He inserts the video, presses play: a Black and Decker being switched on.

You can't see the face, of course, but the hand belongs to one of my group.

Now a shot of a man with insulation tape over his mouth.

The man with the tape over his mouth is someone who failed his test.

The drill is moving towards the man's face.

There is so much fear, so much wanting. But we're all searching.
Searching aren't we?

Exit **Brian**.

Lulu *and* **Robbie** *watch as the video continues.*

Scene Ten

Flat. **Robbie** *is on the phone.*

Robbie   Come on. Take it.
This is . . . it's a golden opportunity. We could change the course of history.

A mobile phone starts to ring. **Lulu** *enters.*

That's what I say. Standing in the Garden and it's: All of humanity, the course of history. / Look, I'm offering it to you. Because we are the first, we are the only ones. And I want you to take it.

Lulu (*on mobile*)   / Hello. Hello, Terry.
No. You call as often as you like.
Oh good. Yes, that's a good idea. A cord that reaches the bed.
Now, if you give me the number again. Yes.
And the expiry date. (*A second mobile rings.*) Yes.
Now I'm taking you into another.
Yes. I'm taking you into the bedroom.

Exit **Lulu**.

Robbie   Here in my hand. Skin. Core. Red. Red skin. And there's juice.
And you see the juice and you want to bite.
Bite. Yes. Your tongue. The apple. Good. The forbidden fruit.

(*Answers second mobile.*) Yes? For the . . . ? If you can . . . ?
She's just. Yes. Coming. On her way. Yes.

(*To phone.*) And it's like you've never seen before, you've never looked at my body.

(*To second mobile.*) If you can wait, if you can hang on.
Because we're really very . . . sure, sure. A couple of minutes.

(*To phone.*) My, my cock. It's hard. And what's there between your . . . yes . . . because oh look you've got one too . . . that you've never noticed . . . yes. Your own big cock.

(*To second mobile.*) Still there? Still holding? So, you're done. Another time. Of course.

(*To phone.*) And you want me and I want you and it's man on man and I'm Adam and you're Adam.

The second mobile starts to ring again.

And you want to take it right up the . . . yes . . . oh yes . . .
/ up against the Tree of Knowledge.

Enter **Lulu**, *still on first mobile*.

Lulu   / Smack. Smack. Smack.
Good. Good. Yes. Yes.

She puts down the first mobile and answers the second mobile.

Hello?
The name?
And the number.
Ah. Gallop. Yes.
Gallop apace you fiery-footed steeds towards Phoebus'
lodging! Such a waggoner as Phaeton would whip . . .
Yes . . .
Spread thy . . .
Good, that's right.
Come, civil night. Come, gentle night. Come, loving black-
browed night. Come, Romeo.
Yes, nearly oh yes.
Oh I have bought the mansion of a love but have not
possessed it, and though I am sold not yet enjoyed.
Dirty fucking cunting fucker.
Yes. Yes. Good. Good. Bye then. Bye.

Robbie (*on phone*)   This is, I tell you this is Paradise. This is
Heaven on the Earth. And the spheres are sphering and the
firm . . .
Good good.
And now we're in the . . . ? Tower of . . . I see . . . the
Tower of Babel. All the tongues in the world. Splashinsky.
Mossambarish. Bam bam bam. Pashka pashka pashka.
Alright then. You're done? Good good. That's good. You
take care now. Yeah.

(*To* **Lulu**.)   Nine hundred pounds and seventy-eight pence.

Lulu   Why are there so many sad people in this world?

Robbie   We're making money.

Lulu   Yeah. Making money.

Robbie   We're gonna be all right.

Scene Eleven

Changing room at Harvey Nichols. **Mark** *is trying on an expensive designer suit.*

Gary (*off*)   How's it going?

Mark   Yeah. Good.

Gary   Do you want the other size?

Mark   No. This is great.

Gary   Alright then.

Mark   Have a look if you like.

Enter **Gary**. *He is transformed: top to toe designer gear and carrying bundles of expensive shopping bags.*

Gary   Oh yes.

Mark   Like it?

Gary   Oh yeah. It's you. Suits you. Do you want it?

Mark   I don't know.

Gary   If you like it, you have it.

Mark   I mean, it's not like I'm ever gonna wear it.

Gary   You don't know that. You're starting over.

Mark   I do like it.

Gary   Could be anything. New life, new gear. It makes sense. Go on.

Mark   You sure you can / afford . . . ?

Gary   Hey. None of that.

Mark   Alright then. Yes.

Gary   Good and now we'll . . .

He holds out a handful of credit cards as if they were playing cards.

Pick a card, any card.

Mark *picks a card. Reads the name on it.*

Mark   P. Harmsden.

Gary   You remember? Last night. Poppers. Kept on hitting himself.

Mark   Ah. P. Harmsden.

Gary   Right then. Get it off and then we're eating out. My treat.

Mark   Why don't you . . . wait outside?

Gary   I'm not bothered.

Mark   Have a look round. I'll only be a few minutes.

Gary   Too late now. I've seen it.

Mark   Seen the . . . ?

Gary   Seen the hard-on.

Mark   Ah yes. The hard-on.

Gary   Must be aching by now. Up all day.
Is it the shopping does that?
You gotta thing about shopping?
Or is it 'cos of me?

Mark   Yes. That's right. It's because of you.

Gary   Right.
What's going on in your head?
I mean, I can see what's going on in your pants but what's in there?
Tell me.

Mark   Nothing. Look. It's just a physical thing, you know?

Gary   So why don't you say what you want. Do you want to kiss me?

Mark   Yes.

Gary   Go on then.

Mark   Listen, if we do . . . anything, it's got to mean nothing, you understand?

Gary   Course.

Mark   If I feel like it's starting to mean something then I'll stop.

Gary   You can kiss me like a gentle kiss. Me mum, she's got a nice kiss.

Mark *kisses* **Gary**.

Gary   How was that?

Mark   Yes. That was alright.

Gary   How old do you think I am?

Mark   I don't know.

Gary   When you met me – what did you think?

Mark   I don't . . . sort of sixteen, seventeen.

Gary   Right. Bit more?

Mark   Bit more.

He kisses **Gary** *again. This time it becomes more sexual. Eventually,* **Mark** *pulls away.*

No. I don't want this.

Gary   I knew it. You've fallen for me.

Mark   Fuck. I really thought I'd broken this, you know?

Gary   Do you love me? Is that what it is? Love?

Mark   I don't know. How would you define that word? There's a physical thing, yes. A sort of wanting which isn't love is it? No, That's well, desire. But then, yes, there's an attachment I suppose. There's also that. Which means I want to be with you, Now, here, when you're with me I feel

like a person and if you're not with me I feel less like a
person.

Gary   So is that love then?
Say what you mean.

Mark   Yes.
I love you.

Gary   See.

Mark   But what I'd like to do – now that I've said that
which was probably very foolish – what I'd like to do is
move forward from this point and try to develop a
relationship that is mutual, in which there's a respect, a
recognition of the other's needs.

Gary   I didn't feel anything.

Mark   No?

Gary   When you kissed me. Nothing.

Mark   I see.

Gary   Which means . . . gives me the power, doesn't it? So
I'll tell you. You're not what I'm after. I don't want it like
that.

Mark   But over a period of time . . .

Gary   No.

Mark   You see, if you've never actually been loved –

Gary   I'm not after love. I want to be owned. I want
someone to look after me. And I want him to fuck me.
Really fuck me. Not like that, not like him. And, yeah, it'll
hurt. But a good hurt.

Mark   But if you had a choice.

Gary   Then I wouldn't choose you. I want to be taken
away. Someone who understands me.

Mark   There's no one out there.

Gary   Think just because you don't feel that way no one else does? There's lots of people who understand. And someone's gonna do it.
I'm going now.

Mark   Stay please. Please I . . .

Mark *kisses* **Gary**, *who pushes him away.*

Gary   That's not true about me mum. I don't let her kiss me. She's a slag.
You go home now. You go back where you belong.

Mark   I want to stay with you.
Give me a day, OK? Another day.

Gary   Don't waste your time with me.

Mark   You can . . . look yes. Come home with me.

Gary   What for? I'm nothing.

Mark   Show you where I live, who I live with.

Gary   You're pathetic you.

Mark   Just one more day. Give it a day.

Gary   You gonna take me home and fuck me?
Alright then. One day. Take me home.

Mark   Suck my cock.

Gary   You taking me home?

Mark   Suck my cock now. Take you home later.

Gary   There's a security camera.

Mark   Doesn't matter.

Gary   All this for me? Fourteen.
You got it wrong. I'm fourteen.

Scene Twelve

Robbie *and* **Lulu** *looking at the phone.*

Robbie   Come on. Ring. Ring.
This shouldn't be happening.
Why is this happening?
I mean, we're close really. Nearly two thousand. Over two
thousand – that's good, isn't it? We're very, very close.
We've been working. We're making money. We're good at
it, aren't we? Isn't that right? You'd say that's right,
wouldn't you?

Lulu   That's right.

Robbie   So, it can't stop now. They've got to keep on
coming.
Ring you bastard ring.
Shit. I can't stand it.

Lulu   It's just quiet. A quiet time. That happens.

Robbie   Hasn't happened before.

Lulu   Sit down. Relax.

Robbie   I can't.

Lulu   It'll start again.

Robbie   There isn't time. We can't afford this.

Lulu   Just a moment's peace. Make the most of it.

Robbie   I want to live. I want to survive, don't you?

Lulu   I don't know.

Robbie   You want to die?

Lulu   No. I want to be free. I don't want to live like this.

Robbie   That's right. Another day yeah?

Lulu   Yes.

Robbie   One more day and we'll be free.

Lulu   Yes.

Robbie   If it keeps on ringing.

Ping of a microwave.

Lulu   Food's ready.

Robbie   Yeah.

Lulu   Eat something?

Robbie   Yes.

Exit **Lulu**.

Robbie   Come on. Come on. Please.

He picks up the phone and speaks into it.

Why aren't you ringing you . . .

He realises that the line is dead.
Checks the lead – finds it's been pulled out of the wall.
Checks the mobiles. They've been switched off.

Sits.

Enter **Lulu** *with microwave meals, offers one to* **Robbie**.

Robbie   No thanks.

Lulu   Eat something.

Robbie   No thanks.

Lulu   Come on.

Robbie   I'm not hungry.

Lulu   Alright then.

Pause.

Have a bit.

Robbie   Don't want any.

Lulu   Might as well have a meal while it's quiet.

Robbie   You reckon?

Lulu   It'll all start again in a minute.

Robbie   They'll all be ringing?

Lulu   Of course.

Robbie   Don't think so. Do you?

Lulu   Course they will.

Robbie   No. I reckon they're not gonna ring. I reckon that tomorrow we're gonna die.

Lulu   Course not.

Robbie   Because I reckon that one of us wants to die.

Lulu   No.

Robbie   No?

Lulu   No.

Robbie   Then tell me why one of us disconnected the phones.

Lulu   For a few moments. I just wanted / a few minutes peace.

Robbie   And I want to live. That's what I want to do.

Lulu   I just wanted to eat a meal without . . . all that.

Robbie   There'll be time later.

Lulu   I can't stand it. In my head.

Robbie   And what about me?
We've got to do this together.

Robbie *moves to reconnect the phone.*

Lulu   No. Please. Not yet.

Robbie   We have to carry on.

Lulu   After we've eaten this. Ten, five minutes.

Robbie   Come on.

Lulu   There was this phone call. I had this call. Twenty minutes, half hour ago. Youngish. Quite well spoken really. And I did the . . . you know . . . where are you sitting? In the living-room. Right. And you're . . . ? Yes, yes, playing with his dick. Good. Fine. So far, auto-pilot. And then he says, I'm watching this video. Well, that's good. And then he starts to . . . he describes . . . because he got this video from his mate who copied it from his mate who copied it from dahdahdah. And I mean, he's wanking to this video of a woman, a student girl who's in the Seven-Eleven, working behind the counter. And there's a wino and . . . yeah.

Robbie   Fuck.

Lulu   Yeah. He was wanking to the video.
So if we can just. A few more minutes.

Robbie   No. We're gonna carry on.

Lulu   Eat something first.

Robbie   There's no time.

Lulu   Eat. Eat. Eat first. Few minutes.

Robbie   I'm not eating.

Lulu   What's wrong with the / . . . Look, if I'm eating . . . If I can . . .

Robbie   I don't want the food, / it doesn't taste of anything . . .

Lulu   And why? / What is so wrong that you can't eat it?

Robbie   I'm not eating. / There isn't time.

Lulu   Come on, you've got the world here. You've got all the tastes in the world. You've got an empire under cellophane. Look, China. India. Indonesia. In the past you'd have to invade, you'd have to occupy just to get one of these things and now, when they're sitting here in front of you, you're telling me you can't taste anything.

Lulu *holds* **Robbie** *back to prevent him reconnecting the phone.*

Robbie   Well, yes. Yes I am. / There's no taste. This stuff tastes of nothing.

Lulu   Eat it. Eat it. Eat it.

Robbie   This stuff?

Lulu   Now. Eat it now.

Robbie   No. This? This is shit. / This? I wouldn't feed a fucking paraplegic with cancer this shit.

Lulu   Eat it. Eat it. Eat it. Eat it.

Lulu *pushes* **Robbie***'s face into the food.*

Enter **Mark** *and* **Gary**.

Mark   Hello.

Robbie   Where have you been?
You went out to get chocolate. A week ago.
Chocolate or a cheeseburger from the shop.
So why have you brought him back?

Mark   Show him where I live.

Robbie   Been shopping? How did you pay for all that?

Mark   He paid.

Gary   Yeah. Paid for everything.

Mark   Who I lived with.

Robbie   And here we are. I'm Barney, this is Betty. Pebbles is playing outside somewhere. And you must be Wayne.

Gary   Wayne? I'm not Wayne. Who's Wayne?

Lulu   We're just eating. Sitting down for a meal. It's actually very difficult to share them actually because they're specifically designed as individual portions but I can get an extra plate. Plate. Knife. Whatever.

Mark   No no no. I don't think we're that hungry.

Robbie   We? We? Listen to that: we.

Mark   Well, I don't think we are.

Gary   Didn't come round to eat, did we?

Mark   No, no, we didn't, no.

Robbie   You on special offer?

Gary   You what?

Robbie   Cheaper than a Twix?

Gary   He don't need to pay me.

Robbie   Really? He will do. He's got this thing. Has to make it a transaction.

Gary   Not with me.

Lulu   It all got a bit messy.

Robbie   Paid Wayne, didn't you?

Mark   Gary, this is Lulu.

Lulu   Things got out of hand.

Gary   Some people you just give it away, don't you?

Lulu   Let's sit down, shall we? Let's all just sit.

They sit.

Well, look at this mess. If you don't watch yourself, you just revert, don't you? To the playground or canteen and suddenly it's all food fights and mess.
So let's be adults. Not much but I think I can still . . . a portion. Anyone?
Darling?

Mark   No.

Robbie   So – you're special?

Gary   He thinks so.

Robbie   He said that? He told you that?

Mark   Come on now. Leave him alone.

Gary   Yes. He said that.

Robbie   Tell me.

Mark (*to* **Robbie**)   Leave him alone.

Robbie   I want to know.

Lulu   Pudding is going to be quite a surprise I can tell you. / I'm really looking forward to pudding.

Robbie   Tell me what he said to you.

Gary   He said: I love you.

Mark   It wasn't those words.

Gary   Yeah, yeah. I love you. I'd be lost without you.

Mark   I never said those words.

Robbie (*to* **Gary**)   You're lying. Fucking lying.

Robbie *leaps on* **Gary** *and starts to strangle him.*

Gary   No. It's true. Please. 'S true. He loves me.

Mark   Leave him alone. Get off. Off.

Mark *attacks* **Robbie**, *who is attacking* **Gary**.
Lulu *tries to protect the ready meals, but most are crushed in the mêlée.*

Lulu   Stop it. Stop. Now.

Mark *succeeds in pulling* **Robbie** *off* **Gary**. *The fight subsides.*

Gary   Loony. You're a fucking headcase, you are.

Lulu   Come on leave it now leave it.

Gary   Fucking going for me.

Lulu   Ssssh . . . quiet . . . quiet.

Long pause.

Robbie   'I love you.'

Lulu   Forget it.

Robbie   That's what he said you said.

Mark   I never said – because – look – I don't.

Exit **Mark**.

Lulu   Mess. Look at this. Why is everything such a mess?

Lulu *scrapes up as much as she can on to the tray and exits.*
Robbie *and* **Gary** *regard each other in silence.*

Gary   He *does* love me. He did say that.

Robbie   Did he do this thing – ask you to lick his balls while he came?

Gary   Yeah. Have you . . . ?

Robbie   Too many times. I'm his boyfriend.

Gary   He doesn't do nothing for me, alright?

Robbie   No? Not your type?

Gary   He's too soft.

Pause.

Do you love him?

Robbie   Yes.

Pause.

Gary   It's all gentle with him. That's not what I'm after. Got to find this bloke. I know he's out there. Just got to find him.

Robbie   Someone who's not gentle?

Gary   Yeah, something strong. Firm, you know.

Robbie   Yes.

Gary   You think he's cruel but really he's looking out for you. I'm going to be somewhere. I'll be dancing. Shopping. Whatever. And he'll fetch me. Take me away.

Robbie   If he exists.

Gary   You what?

Robbie   If he really exists.

Gary   You saying I'm lying?

Robbie   I didn't say that.
I think . . . I think we all need stories, we make up stories so that we can get by.
And I think a long time ago there were big stories. Stories so big you could live your whole life in them. The Powerful Hands of the Gods and Fate. The Journey to Enlightenment. The March of Socialism. But they all died or the world grew up or grew senile or forgot them, so now we're all making up our own stories. Little stories. It comes out in different ways. But we've each got one.

Gary   Yes.

Robbie   It's lonely. I understand. But you're not alone. I could help. I'm offering to help. Where you gonna start? Maybe I know what you're looking for.

Gary   A helping hand. What do you wanna do that for?

Robbie   For a fee.

Gary   Yeah?

Robbie   Yeah. Pay me and you'll get what you want. I've got instincts. I know about this other bloke.

Gary   If I get what I want.

Robbie   Cash. It's got to be cash.

Gary   Course.

Robbie   You've got the money?

Gary   Yeah. I've got the money.
So. What you gonna do? To help me.

Robbie   We're gonna play a game.

Scene Thirteen

The flat.

Mark, **Gary**, **Lulu** *and* **Robbie**.

Mark   Why are we playing this?

Robbie   Because he wants to.

Mark   It's a stupid game.

Robbie   Your friend. Isn't that right?

Gary   Right.

Mark   Why do you want to play this?

Gary   In my head, I see this picture, alright?

Lulu   Yes.

Gary   Well, like a picture but like a story, you know?

Robbie   Yes?

Gary   A sort of story of pictures.

Lulu   A film?

Gary   Yeah, story like a film.

Robbie   With you?

Gary   Yes.

Lulu   You're in the film?

Gary   Yes.

Robbie   You're the hero – ?

Gary   Well –

Lulu   You're the protag – you are the central character of the film?

Gary   Sort of. Yeah.

Robbie   Right.

Gary   So there's this story, film and I – there's these stairs.

Pause.

Robbie   What?

Gary   No. Look, I don't want to . . .

Lulu   You don't want to –

Gary   I thought I could but I can't, alright?
It's just saying it. Sorry.

Robbie   So – just wasting our time?

Gary   I'm sorry.

Robbie   We should have got the money first.

Lulu   You're not going through with this?

Gary   I don't know.

Robbie   He should have paid up front.

Mark   Paying for . . . ?

Robbie   Paying to play the game.

Lulu   So do you want to do this?

Pause.

Robbie   Pointless. Wasting our time. I mean, how old are you? What are you? Some kid wasting our time.

Gary   I'm not a kid.

Robbie   You don't know what you want.

Gary   I know what I want.

Lulu   So . . . ?

Gary It's just . . . the words. It's describing it.

Mark Alright. Come back to him.

Robbie Now, as I'm the judge –

Mark Do me. Ask me – truth or dare?

Robbie That's not fair. That's not in the rules, is it?

Mark But if he's not ready.

Robbie Right. A forfeit. Something I'd like you to . . . something by way of punishment.

Mark Just leave it, OK?

Gary Shit, I don't want to.

Robbie (*to* **Lulu**) What do you think would be a suitable punishment?

Mark (*to* **Gary**) It's alright. It's alright.

Gary Shit.

Gary*'s tears are close to hysteria.*

Mark I'll do it. We can come back to you.
Now – ask me a question.

Robbie No.

Mark Come on – ask me a question.

Lulu Alright.

Robbie It's cheating.

Lulu I know. My question is . . . My question is: who is the most famous person you've ever fucked?

Mark The most famous person?

Lulu The most famous person.

Mark Well OK then OK.

Robbie If you're gonna . . . it's got to be the truth.

Mark   Yeah, yeah.

Robbie   Or it doesn't count.

Mark   I know.

Lulu   Come on. The most famous person.

Robbie   No because last time –

Lulu   Come on.

Robbie   No because before.

Lulu   Let him say it.

Robbie   You made it up last time.

Mark   I know, I know.

Robbie   So what I'm saying is –

Mark   I know what you're saying.

Robbie   I'm saying it's got to be true.

Mark   Right.

Beat.

Robbie   Right.

Beat.

Lulu   Well then –

Mark   Well then. I'm in Tramps, OK? Tramps or Annabel's, OK?

Robbie   Which – ?

Mark   I can't remember.

Robbie   Look, you've got to –

Lulu   Go on.

Mark   Tramps or Annabel's or somewhere, OK?

Robbie   If you don't know where.

Mark It doesn't matter where, OK?

Robbie If it's true then –

Mark The place, the name doesn't matter.

Lulu No. It doesn't matter.

Robbie I think you should know –

Mark What the fuck does it matter where?

Lulu Alright.

Mark When what you said was who.

Lulu Come on. Who? Who? Who?

Mark Tramps or Annabel's or someplace. Someplace because the place is not of importance, OK? Because the place doesn't matter. So I'm at this somewhere place –

Robbie When?

Mark Jesus.

Lulu It doesn't matter.

Robbie I want to know when.

Lulu Come on, you're there and –

Robbie I want to know when?

Mark Sometime. In the past.

Robbie The last week past? The last year past? Your childhood past?

Lulu The past past.

Mark Well I don't –

Robbie Come on –

Lulu Why?

Robbie Veracity. For the /

Mark / alright then alright /

Robbie   / veracity of it.

Mark   '84. '85. About then. OK?

Robbie   OK.

Mark   So I'm in this place – which is maybe Tramps maybe not – and it's possibly 1985 –

Robbie   That's all I wanted to know.

Mark   I'm having a good time.

Robbie   Meaning?

Mark   Meaning a good time. Meaning a time that is good.

Robbie   Meaning you've taken –

Mark   Meaning I'm having a time that is good.

Robbie   Because you've taken –

Mark   Not necessarily.

Robbie   But you had?

Mark   I don't know.

Robbie   Come on. '84. '85. You must have been on something.

Mark   Well yes.

Robbie   Yes.

Mark   Probably yes.

Robbie   Because really when can you say you're not –

Mark   What? Go on, what?

Robbie   When can you say you're not on something?

Mark   Now.

Robbie   Yeah?

Lulu   Come on. Come on.

Robbie   You're sure? Sure that you're not –

Mark   Yes.

Lulu   Let's – the story.

Mark   I'm fucking clean, alright?

Lulu   Come on. '84. '85. Tramps. Annabel's.

Robbie   Yeah. Right.

Mark   I mean, what the fuck do I have to – ? I'm clean, OK?

Lulu   Please. I want to know who.

Mark   Alright. Just don't – alright. Tramps. '84. I'm having a good time.

Robbie   You're tripping?

Mark   No. And I need a piss, yes?

Lulu   In the toilet?

Mark   Yes, a piss in the toilet.

Lulu   This is a toilet story.

Mark   So, I'm taking my way to the toilet, right? And there's this woman, OK? This woman is like watching me.

Lulu   Who? Who? Who?

Mark   Of course, I should have known then. I should have known who she was.

Lulu   Who?

Mark   But I mean I am so –

Robbie   You're tripping.

Mark   No.

Robbie   You should have known who she was but you're tripping.

Mark   Look, I was not tripping.

Robbie   You didn't recognise this famous person because you were completely out of it.

Mark   OK, OK, I was completely out of it.

Lulu   And you're on your way to the toilet.

Mark   Out of it. All I know is that this woman's eyes are like: give me your veiny bang stick, OK?

Lulu   Way with words.

Mark   So I'm pissing. Urinals. I'm pissing in the urinals and in the mirror I can see the door, OK? Well, OK. Pissing and the door opens. Door opens and it's her.

Lulu   So you're what – in the ladies?

Robbie   Urinals in the ladies?

Mark   Nope.

Robbie   So this is the –

Mark   Urinals in the gents.

Robbie   So she's –

Mark   She's there in the gents, OK? Standing in the gents watching me piss, OK? And now, we're in like bright – we're in fluorescent light I see.

Lulu   Who? Who? Who?

Mark   Not yet.

Robbie   Why not?

Mark   Because I'm out of it, OK. As you say, I'm on something. I should know who, but I don't recognise her, OK?

Lulu   So then bright light and you see . . . ?

Mark   See what she's wearing. A uniform. She is wearing a police uniform.

Lulu   Fuck. Who? Who? Who?

Robbie   A man's uniform or – ?

Mark   WPC. The Docs, the stockings, the jacket. The works. The hat. And she looks me in the eyes –

Gary   A woman?

Robbie   You're pissing?

Mark   Looks me in the eyes by way of the mirror, OK?

Robbie   OK, OK.

Gary   You did it with a woman?

Mark   She looks, she, she, she cruises me and then goes into one of the cubicles but looking at me all the time, you know? Goes into one of the cubicles and leaves the door ajar. I want to race right in there, you know? Get down to it but, like you do, I count to ten. Count to ten and then like coolly walk past. And as I walk past I take a cool glance to my left, cool look into the cubicle, cubicle with the door ajar and – wow.

Lulu   Wow?

Mark   Wow? The skirt is up around the waist. The skirt is up and the knickers are off or maybe she never had knickers – who knows? – but the skirt is up and she is like displaying this beautiful, come and get it snatch to die for, OK?

Gary   Said you didn't go for women.

Robbie   Facing / you?

Lulu   Who is it?

Mark   So I'm in there. I'm in and I kneel. I pay worship. My tongue is worshipping that pussy like it's God. And that's when she speaks. Speaks and I know who she is.

Lulu   Who?

Mark   She says 'Oh yah. Chocks away.'

Lulu   No.

Robbie   What?

Gary   Is this a woman?

Lulu   No – it can't be.

Robbie   I told you.

Lulu   That is fucking unbelievable.

Robbie   Yes, yes it is.

Lulu   What? Fergie?

Mark   Yup. Fergie.

Lulu   Fucking hell.

Mark   I recognise the voice. Get a look at the face. It's her.

Robbie   Come on –

Mark   Fergie is like 'chocks away'. Fergie is right down to it. Fergie is ready to swallow anything, you know? I mean, any chocks there might have been have been chocked away. So a couple of minutes later, I'm there and Fergie is fellating. It's gobbledeygobble up against the cistern.

Robbie   Nobody believes this. How can you believe this?

Mark   Gobbledeygobble and the door, door to the cubicle starts to open.

Robbie   This is ridiculous.

Mark   I haven't locked the door, you see.

Robbie   We said the truth. It had to be the truth.

Mark   Rule number one. Always lock the door.

Robbie   No one believes this.

Mark   Door opens and there's another woman. Yes.
There's a second woman. Another policewoman like
squeezes her way in.

Robbie   Shut up.

Mark   With blonde hair.

Robbie   SHUT UP. SHUT THE FUCK UP.

Pause.

Mark   What? What I thought you wanted to know . . .

Robbie   The truth.

Mark   Which is what . . .

Robbie   No.
(*To* **Lulu**.) Do you believe him?
(*To* **Gary**.) Do you?

Pause.

Rule number one. Never believe a junkie.
Because a junkie is a cunt. And when a junkie looks you in
the eyes and says 'I love you' that's when you know he's
gonna fill you full of shit.

Pause.

Gary   Why didn't you tell me you'd done it with a woman?

Robbie (*to* **Gary**)   Back to you.

Gary   Alright.

Robbie   It's your turn now.

Mark   You don't have to –

Gary   I want to.

Lulu   We'll help you.

Gary   Yeah?

Lulu   Help you find the words.

Robbie   Alright then. Alright. Your story. Your film, yeah?

Gary   Yeah.

Robbie   I think I know what it is. I see. I understand.

Gary   Yeah.

Robbie   Yes. These pictures in your head.

So if I help – yes? If I can help you to describe the pictures then –

Gary   Yes.

Robbie   Alright. Alright. There's you yes and you're.
I see you . . . there's music yes?

Gary   Music. Yes.

Robbie   Loud music. Dum dum dum. Like / techno.

Gary   Techno music. Yes.

Robbie   Techno music and you're moving like – you're dancing yes?

Gary   Dancing.

Robbie   Dancing on a dance floor. Dance floor in a club.

Gary   Yes. Yes. A club.

Robbie   And you're dancing with this bloke.

Gary   No. Not like that. He's just there.

Robbie   Dancing by yourself. But now . . .

Gary   Watching.

Robbie   Bloke who's watching you.

Gary   I'm dancing.

Lulu   He's watching.

Gary   Yeah. Watching me.

Lulu   And you smile.

Gary No. No smile.

Robbie But you know, you think: you don't have a choice.

Lulu No control.

Gary No control.

Robbie Because he's . . .

Lulu Because he's . . .

Gary Because he's gonna / take me away.

Robbie Have you. I'm going to have you.

Lulu He's going to have you.

Mark Come on, leave –

Robbie No.

Mark This is – it's getting heavy.

Gary No.

Robbie We're getting to the truth.

Gary I want to do it.

Lulu Now there's another – a fat bloke.

Gary Yes? A fat bloke?

Lulu Fat bloke who owns you.

Gary I didn't know about him.

Lulu Owns you but doesn't want you.
And the fat bloke says:
See that one dancing?

Robbie Yeah. Yeah. I see him.

Lulu Well, he's mine. I own him.

Mark Fuck's sake.

Lulu I own him but I don't want him.

Gary   Dunt want me.

Lulu   You know something.
He's trash and I hate him.

Robbie   Hate him.

Gary   Right. Hates me.

Robbie   And the fat bloke says –

Lulu   Well, you wanna buy him?

Gary   Yes.

Robbie   And / I say.

Gary   You say.

Robbie   How much?

Lulu   Piece of trash like that. Well, let's say twenty. He's yours for twenty.

Robbie   So you see the money.

Gary   I see money. See you pay him.

Robbie   You've seen the . . .

Gary   Transaction. I've seen the transaction.

Robbie   Transaction.

Gary   Yes and you've come to fetch me. You don't say anything. Just take me away.

Robbie   Good. Take you away.

Gary   Big car. Through the security gates and we're in the house.
And now dark. I can't see because . . . I'm wearing a, there's like a . . .

Lulu   A blindfold?

Gary   Blindfold. Yes . . . like a blindfold.

Lulu *produces a blindfold.*

Mark *pushes* **Lulu** *away and put his arms around* **Gary**.

Mark   Alright. Stop now. See? You can choose this instead. You must like that.
Just to be loved.

Gary   What are you doing?

Mark   Just holding you.

Gary   You've not even fucked me.

He pushes **Mark** *away.*

You're taking the piss, aren't you?

Mark   I'm just trying to show you. Because, I don't think that you have ever actually been loved and if the world has offered us no practical . . .

Gary   What are you?

Mark   I can take care of you.

Gary   You're nobody. You're not what I want.

Mark   If you can just get out of this trap.

Gary   I don't want you. Understand? You're nothing.

Mark   Wait. I just need to get this.

Mark *takes coke from* **Gary**'*s pocket and retreats.*

Lulu   Do you understand what we're going to do to you?

Gary   Yes.

Lulu   You understand and do you want us to do this?

Gary   Yes.

Lulu *puts the blindfold on* **Gary**.

Robbie   Blindfold you and –

Gary   Take me up the stairs.

Robbie   In my house?

Gary   In your house.

Lulu *and* **Robbie** *spin* **Gary** *around.*

Robbie   And you feel . . . you know this house. Know you've been here before.

Gary   Yeah. When have I been here before?

Lulu   And now. Now a bare room.
So – you're the new slave?

Robbie   Yes. Yes, old woman. This is the new slave.

Lulu   Beware. Beware. Do you know what the last slave died of?

Gary   No. There's no woman.

Robbie   Now.

Lulu   Sssssh. He's coming. The master is coming. Ssssssshhh.

Gary   I know this house. I know who he is.

Robbie   Knob. Knob on the door turning.

Silence. **Gary** *stands very still.* **Robbie** *slowly approaches him from behind. Long pause –* **Robbie** *inches away from* **Gary**.

Gary   Go on.

Robbie   Yes?

Gary   Do it.

Robbie   It's what you want.

Gary   Yes.

Robbie *starts to undo* **Gary**'s *trousers.*

Robbie   Yes?

Gary   Yes.

Robbie *pulls down* **Gary**'s *trousers.*

He spits on his hand. Slowly he works the spit up **Gary**'s *arse.*

Robbie   Now?

Gary   Do it now.

Robbie   Now.

Robbie *unzips his fly. Works spit on to his penis. He penetrates* **Gary**. *He starts to fuck him.*

Silence. **Robbie** *continues to fuck* **Gary**.

Lulu   Is that good? Do you like that?

More silent fucking.

Robbie (*to* **Mark**)   Do you want him?

Mark   I . . .

Robbie   Do you know what he is? Trash. Trash and I hate him. Want him, you can have him.

Mark   Yes.

Robbie *pulls away.* **Mark** *goes through the same routine – spitting and penetrating* **Gary**. *He fucks him viciously.*

Mark   Fuck you. Fuck you.

Lulu   Does it hurt? Is it hurting you?

Gary   Are you him? Are you my dad?

Mark   No.

Gary   Yes. You're my dad.

Mark   I told you – no.

He hits **Gary**.
Then, he pulls away from **Gary**.

Gary   See. See. I know who you are. So finish it.

Mark   No.

He hits **Gary** *repeatedly.*

I'm. Not. Your. Dad.

Lulu   Leave him. Leave him now. Finished. It's over.

Gary   No. Don't stop now.

Robbie   No?

Robbie *gets into position to continue fucking* **Gary**.

Gary   Because – look – this bit. It doesn't end like this.
He's always got something. He gets me in the room,
blindfolds me. But he doesn't fuck me. Well not him, not his
dick. It's the knife. He fucks me – yeah – but with a knife.
So . . .

Pause.

Lulu   No.

Mark   Gotta have something.

Gary   In the kitchen. Or, or a screwdriver. Or something.

Lulu   No.

Gary   Got to be fucking something. That's how it ends.

Robbie *pulls off* **Gary**'s *blindfold.*

Robbie   No. I can't do that.

Gary   You're not gonna finish like this?

Robbie   I'm not gonna do that.

Lulu   You'll bleed.

Gary   Yeah.

Lulu   You could die.

Gary   No. I'll be OK. Promise.

Robbie   It'll kill you.

Gary   It's what I want.

Lulu   Go home now.

Gary Just do it. Just fucking do it.
You're losers – you're fucking losers you know that?

Robbie Yeah.

Gary Listen, right. When someone's paying, someone
wants something and they're paying, then you do it.
Nothing right. Nothing wrong. It's a deal. So then you do it.
I thought you were for real.
Pretending, isn't it? Just a story.

Robbie Yes. It's just a story.

Mark (*to* **Robbie** *and* **Lulu**)   Please leave us now.

Lulu We needed his money.

Mark I know. If you leave us alone. I'll take care of this.
Yes?

Lulu Come on, come on.

Exit **Robbie** *and* **Lulu**.

Gary Are you gonna do it? I want you to do it. Come on.
You can do it.
Because he's not out there.
I've got this unhappiness. This big sadness swelling like it's
gonna burst.
I'm sick and I'm never going to be well.

Mark I know.

Gary I want it over. And there's only one ending.

Mark I understand.

Gary He's got no face in the story. But I want to put a
face to him. Your face.

Mark Yes.

Gary Do it. Do it and I'll say 'I love you'.

Mark Alright. You're dancing and I take you away.

Scene Fourteen

The flat.

Brian *has the holdall of money.*

Brian   You know, life is hard. On this planet. Intractable.
I can tell you this because I feel it. Yes, like you I have felt
this. We work, we struggle. And we find ourselves asking:
what is this for? Is there meaning? I know you've . . . I can
see this question in your eyes. You ask yourself these
questions. Right now – yes?

Robbie   Yes.

Brian   And you – what is there to guide me on my lonely
journey?
Yes?

Lulu   Yes.

Brian   We need something. A guide. A talisman. A set of
rules. A compass to steer us through this everlasting night.
Our youth is spent searching for this guide until we . . .
some give up. Some say there is nothing. There is chaos. We
are born into chaos. But this is . . . no. This is too painful.
This is too awful to contemplate. This we deny. Am I right?

Robbie   Yes.

Brian   Yes. I have a rung a bell. Good, good. Bells are
rung.
Chaos or . . . order. Meaning. Something that gives us
meaning.

Pause.

My dad once said to me. My dad said it to me and now I'm
going to say it to you. One day my dad says to me: Son,
what are the first few words in the Bible?

Robbie   In the beginning.

Brian   No.

Robbie Yes. In the beginning.

Brian I'm telling you no.

Robbie That's what it says. In the beginning.

Brian No, son. I'm telling you no. And you listen to me when I'm telling you no, alright?

Robbie Alright.

Brian Tell me, son, says my dad, what are the first few words in the Bible? I don't know, Dad, I say, what are the first few words in the Bible? And he looks at me, he looks me in the eye and he says: Son, the first few words in the Bible are . . . get the money first. Get. The Money. First.

Pause.

It's not perfect, I don't deny it. We haven't reached perfection. But it's the closest we've come to meaning, Civilisation is money. Money is civilisation. And civilisation – how did we get here? By war, by struggle, kill or be killed. And money – it's the same thing, you understand? The getting is cruel, is hard, but the having is civilisation. Then we are civilised. Say it. Say it with me. Money is . . .

Pause.

SAY IT. Money is . . .

Lulu *and* **Robbie** Civilisation.

Brian Yes. Yes. I'm teaching. You're learning. Money is civilisation. And civilisation is . . . SAY IT. Don't get frightened now. And civilisation is . . .

Lulu *and* **Robbie** Money.

Brian *offers them the holdall.*

Brian Here. Take it.

Lulu You . . . ?

Brian I want you to take it.

Lulu   It's all there.

Brian   Yes.

Lulu   Look – if you want to count it. Three thousand.

Brian   Take it from me when I tell you to take it.

Lulu *takes the bag.*

Brian   Good. Good. You see? Do you understand? I am returning the money. You see?

Lulu   I . . . yes.

Brian   And now – you have a question. Ask me the question. Please. Ask the question?

Lulu   Why?

Brian   If you formulate the question . . .

Lulu   Why didn't you take the money? Why did you give us back the money?

Brian   And now I can answer you. I answer. Because you have learnt. The lesson has been learnt you see. You understand this (*Indicates the money.*) and you are civilised. And so – I return it. I give it to you.

Lulu   Thank you.

Brian *gets up, moves to video player. He ejects the video of his son. Takes another video from his pocket. Places it in the machine. Pushes play.*

Lulu (*TV*)   One day we'll know what all this was for, all this suffering, there'll be no more mysteries, but until then we have to carry on living . . . we must work, / that's all we can do. I'm leaving by myself tomorrow, I'll teach in a school, and devote my whole life to people who need it. It's autumn now, it'll soon be winter, and there'll be snow everywhere but I'll be working . . . yes, working.

Brian   We must work.
What we've got to do is make the money. For them. My

boy. Generations to come. We won't see it of course – that purity. But they will. Just as long as we keep on making the money.

Not in chemicals. Not pure. Supplies aren't the best. So a kid dies. And then it's headlines and press conferences. And you watch the dad, you watch a grown man cry and you think: time to move out of chemicals.

He pauses the tape.

That's the future, isn't it? Shopping, Television.
And now you've proved yourselves, I'd like you to join us. All of you. Think about it.

He moves to the exit.

Our second favourite bit was the end. Because by then he's got married. And he's got a kid of his own. Right at the end he stands alone. He's on a rock and he looks up at the night, he looks up at the stars and he says: 'Father. Everything is alright, Father. I remembered. The Cycle of Being.' Or words to that effect.
You ought to see it. You'd like it.

Exit **Brian**. **Mark** *comes forward.*

Mark   It's three thousand AD. Or something. It's the future. The Earth has died. Died or we killed it. The ozone, the bombs, a meteorite. It doesn't matter. But humanity has survived. A few of us . . . jumped ship. And on we go.
So it's three thousand and blahdeblah and I'm standing in the market, some sort of bazaar. A little satellite circling Uranus. Market day. And I'm looking at this mutant. Some of them, the radiation it's made them so ugly, twisted. But this one. Wow. It's made him . . . he's tanned and blond and there's pecs and his dick . . . I mean, his dick is three-foot long.
This fat sort of ape-thing comes up to me and says . . . See the mute with the three-foot dick?
Yeah. I see him.
Well, he's mine and I own him. I own him but I hate him. If I don't sell him today I'm gonna kill him.

So . . . a deal is struck, a transaction, I take my mutant
home and I get him home and I say:
I'm freeing you. I'm setting you free. You can go now. And
he starts to cry. I think it's gratitude. I mean, he should be
grateful but it's . . .
He says – well, he telepathises into my mind – he doesn't
speak our language – he tells me:
Please. I'll die. I don't know how to . . . I can't feed myself.
I've been a slave all my life. I've never had a thought of my
own. I'll be dead in a week.
And I say: That's a risk I'm prepared to take.

Robbie   Thirty-six inches and no shag?

Mark   That's right.

Lulu   I like that ending.

Robbie   It's not bad.

Mark   It's the best I can do.

Robbie   Hungry now? I want you to try some. (*Of the ready
meal.*)

He feeds **Mark** *with a fork.*

Nice?

Mark   Mmmmm.

Robbie   Now give him some of yours.

Lulu   Do you want some?

She feeds **Mark**.

Is that good?

Mark   Delicious.

Robbie   You've got a bit of blood.

Lulu   Bit more?

Mark   Why not?

Lulu *feeds him.*

Robbie   My turn.

Robbie *feeds* **Mark**.

Mark, **Robbie** *and* **Lulu** *take it in turns to feed each other as the lights fade to black.*

Notes

page

Cast list: Robbie, Mark and Gary are named after Robbie Williams, Mark Owen and Gary Barlow, members of Take That, the most influential boy band of the 1990s. Lulu is perhaps named after the Scottish singer Lulu who made a guest appearance on their single 'Relight My Fire' (October 1993), though Ravenhill had also recently adapted Frank Wedekind's 'Lulu plays' for BBC Radio. Brian is perhaps named after Brian Harvey, the lead singer of East 17, Take That's main rival boy band.

5 *Scag*: colloquial term for heroin.

8 *The Lion King*: Disney cartoon movie, released in 1994, directed by Roger Allers and Rob Minkoff. It tells the story of Simba, a lion prince whose father, King Mafusa, is killed (crushed in a stampede, as Brian so nearly says). The killer is Simba's uncle, Scar, who also drives the young lion cub from the kingdom. When Simba is visited by the ghost of his father, he resolves to return and claim his rightful place as lion king. The film mixes Shakespearean resonances, African mythology and lightweight pop (composed by Elton John and Tim Rice). The motifs of fatherhood and violence offer one reason for its inclusion in here, though Ravenhill was also amused by the film's covert homophobia: the film's villain is voiced by Jeremy Irons, in a waspishly effete drawl.

9 *Cycle of Being (words to that effect)*: as always, Brian has slightly misremembered the film, which in fact talks (and sings) of a 'Circle of Life'.

10 *Our viewers*: it transpires that Lulu is auditioning for a shopping channel of the kind that sprang up after the introduction of satellite broadcasting in Britain in 1989.

11 *One day people will know what all this was for*: Lulu is performing Irina's last speech from Chekhov's *Three Sisters*. Like *Shopping and Fucking*, Chekhov's play focuses on a small group of self-obsessed young people with very little self-knowledge.

15 *three hundred E*: ecstasy tablets, which are based on MDMA (3–4 methylenedioxymethamphetamine) a drug that produces rushes of exhilaration and wellbeing, followed by a sustained euphoric, 'blissed out', empathetic state and is much associated with the club scene since the 'summer of love' of 1988. The drug has been illegal since 1985.

17 *Commit myself so quickly to . . . intimacy*: in this scene, and for much of the rest of the play, Mark's words are a pastiche of 1990s therapy-speak. It is important to recognise the absurdity of much that he says and to question whether it is appropriate to think of love and friendship as dangerous addictions. See, for example, his speech on pp. 32–3.
Smack: colloquial term for heroin.
Did you use?: Robbie is asking if Mark was chucked out of the clinic for taking heroin.
I'm clean: Mark is insisting that he has stopped taking heroin and is no longer addicted.

19 *I wanted to . . . lick it*: the sexual activity of penetrating the anus with one's tongue is sometimes known as rimming, sometimes as analingus. Here and in Scene Four, Ravenhill is deliberately using the fact that Mark pays to perform this act in order to evoke the mythical connection between money and shit, a connection that Sigmund Freud famously wrote about in his essay 'Character and Anal Eroticism' (1908).

22 *holograph*: the word means 'signature'. Gary probably means

'hologram', though there's an irony here because Gary does appear to want something more personal than the euphoric cybercommunication he speculates about, and we could see signatures as more personal than holograms.

on the lines: Mark has met Gary through a telephone sex line, typically premium-rate telephone lines staffed by sex workers and designed to help the caller bring him or herself to orgasm. Robbie and Lulu set up a phone sex company in Scene Ten.

23 *How old do you want me to be?*: Gary thinks Mark wants to engage in sexual role-play, perhaps of an older man and younger boy.

knocky: a slang term for 'bad-tempered', like 'narky'. The word is not widespread and may only have been in use in Ravenhill's school in Haywards Heath, West Sussex.

24 *God Squad*: derogatory slang term for a religious zealot, usually Christian.

druggies: slang term for drug users.

26 *There's blood around his mouth*: Gary's arse is bleeding, perhaps due to being anally raped as he describes in Scene Six.

28 *Seven-Eleven*: American chain of convenience stores dating back to the 1920s, that first opened in Britain in 1971. The name is meant to refer to the opening hours.

Wino: derogatory slang term for a homeless alcoholic.

29 *they've made the choice on TV guides so fucking difficult*: under the Broadcasting Act 1990, the monopoly that television companies used to exercise on publishing their own TV listings was broken, which led to a bewildering proliferation of TV listings magazines.

31 *bum-bag*: small bag or pouch attached to a belt and worn around the waist.

33 *I traded. I made money. Tic Tac*: Mark is recalling working in the City of London, probably at the Liffe (London International Financial Futures and Options Exchange) where, in the 'open-

outcry' system in use until 1999, traders used a complex series of hand signals and calls to make deals. This resembles in some way the system of hand signals used by bookmakers to communicate odds at a horse race, known as 'Tic Tac'. The practice has been replaced by electronic communication in the Stock Exchange and the Liffe, but still continues at the International Petroleum Exchange.

34   *cathode rays*: until the invention of plasma screens, cathode ray tubes was the technology behind all televisions. It is unclear why Mark mentions them, except that the word 'ray' sounds menacing, and he may be confusing cathode rays with something else.

madcow: 'Mad Cow Disease' or BSE (Bovine Spongiform Encephalopathy), to give its more formal name, is a fatal degenerative disease of cattle that can spread to humans in the form of vCJD (variant Creutzfeldt-Jacob Disease). The recent epidemic in British cattle which first manifested in 1986 is thought to have been produced by feeding cows with a cattle feed that contained remnants of butchered animals. The crisis was particularly intense in the mid-nineties, with millions of cattle slaughtered to prevent the spread of the disease.

Pot Noodle: a very cheap instant meal, not usually considered haute cuisine.

TCP: an antiseptic liquid.

39   *Rwanda . . . Kiev . . . Bogata*: in Rwanda in 1994 almost a million people were killed in a wave of genocidal slaughter mainly perpetrated by the majority ethnic group, the Hutus, against the minority Tutsis. Kiev is the capital city of the Ukraine which gained independence after the collapse of the Soviet Union in 1991 and immediately entered an era of economic decline and galloping inflation. Bogata is the capital of Colombia, which had seen a decade of bloody struggles between the government, drug cartels, guerillas and paramilitary groups.

Pillowbiter. Shitstabber: derogatory slang terms for homosexual men, deriving from imagined scenes of anal intercourse.

50 In the original Out of Joint production, the interval was taken between Scenes Nine and Ten.

Standing in the Garden: Lulu and Robbie's phone sex role-plays take mythically famous stories and turn them, obscurely at times, into erotic scenarios. The first is the story of Adam and Eve in the Garden of Eden, as told in Genesis 1–3, the first book of the Bible, where Eve tempts Adam to eat the forbidden fruit of the Tree of the Knowledge of Good and Evil.

52 *Gallop apace you fiery-footed steeds*: Lulu is enacting sexual role-play based on Shakespeare's *Romeo and Juliet*. The words she uses, in the order they appear in her speech, are to be found in Act Three, Scene Two, ll. 1–3, 10, 20, 17, 26–8.

Tower of Babel: the story, which appears in Genesis 11, is that originally there was only one language on the earth until an attempt was made to build a tower reaching up to the heavens. God saw the dangers of humanity's unfettered ambition and multiplied their languages so that no one could understand anyone else.

53 *Harvey Nichols*: luxurious department store in Knightsbridge, London.

54 *Poppers*: alkyl nitrites, illegal as a stimulant. They come in small bottles of liquid and a short sniff of the vapours causes a rush of oxygen to the head, sexual stimulation and muscle relaxation. They are sometimes used by gay men during anal sex.

61 *auto-pilot*: a navigational device to keep planes on course without the human pilot's intervention, used often as a metaphor for behaving automatically without having consciously to make decisions.

62 *I'm Barney, this is Betty. Pebbles is playing outside somewhere*: Barney and Betty are a married couple in the American cartoon series *The Flintstones*, and Pebbles is their pet dinosaur. *The*

Flintstones was a cartoon version of the very conventional families common to American television comedy in the 1950s and 60s.

66   *Enlightenment*: a period in Western thinking during the eighteenth century characterised by a belief in human reason, progress, universal human rights and duties, scientific method, and the perfectability of society and humanity. Some think that nowadays we can no longer believe in such things.

The March of Socialism: the progress of socialism, the belief that society should be run for the common good, that inequalities should be constrained, and that capitalism is fundamentally incompatible with human freedom. Some think that nowadays we can no longer believe in such things.

67   *stupid game*: they are playing Truth or Dare, a game in which the players are obliged to answer personal questions or else do something of the other players' choice. In Jay McInerney's *Story of My Life*, a significant influence on the writing of *Shopping and Fucking*, the heroine Alison Poole plays this game at a key moment in the book (Chapter Ten).

70   *Tramps*: London nightclub on Jermyn Street, irreversibly associated with the 1980s.

Annabel's: upper-class London nightclub in Berkeley Square, still firmly associated with the 1980s, famous for the night in June 1986 when Princess Diana and Sarah Ferguson ('Fergie', Prince Andrew's fiancée) gate-crashed his stag night dressed as policewomen, the event that forms the basis for Mark's own story.

74   *veiny bang stick*: a humorous term for an erect penis.

78   *Techno music*: a general term for electronically-produced dance music.

86   *the first few words in the Bible*: . . . are actually 'In the beginning God created the heaven and the earth' (Genesis 1), though Brian's own curious paraphrase is meant to indicate the primacy of economic transactions in all that we do. 'Get the money first' is

reputedly the advice given by Jack Kennedy to his son (and future president) John F. Kennedy.

89 *Our second favourite bit was the end*: Brian is returning to his pleasure at watching *The Lion King* (see note to p. 8).

Questions for Further Study

1   Do you think this play approves of the behaviour and attitudes of its characters?

2   What is the significance of 'stories' in *Shopping and Fucking*?

3   How often in the play is shopping coupled with fucking? Do any patterns emerge that tell us something about the play's view of our world?

4   Discuss the different attitudes to contemporary technology expressed in this play.

5   Is it difficult to identify the sexuality of these characters (gay, straight, bisexual)? How significant is this?

6   What do you think has happened to Gary between Scenes Thirteen and Fourteen? Discuss the significance of each different scenario to our (moral and artistic) evaluation of the play.

7   'The audience is asked to view the text in such a way that the effect is a bit like being at a peep show' (Caridad Svich, 'Commerce and Morality in the Theatre of Mark Ravenhill', *Contemporary Theatre Review*, xiii, 1 (2003), p. 83). How does this play want us to react to its depictions of sex and violence?

8   'The surprising persistence of blood is a running motif in the play' (David Ian Rabey, *English Drama Since 1940,* London, Longman, 2003, p. 201). Why do you think this could be described as surprising? What do the images of blood (and the

reactions of the characters to blood) tell us about the attitudes expressed in and by the play?

9 Mark wants an answer to the question 'Are there any feelings left?' (p. 34). Why does he ask this question? What answer do you think he receives?

10 What is the function of the other texts – *The Lion King*, Chekhov's *Three Sisters, Romeo and Juliet*, Genesis – that appear in the play?

11 Mark believes that he has 'a tendency to define myself purely in terms of my relationship to others' (pp. 32–3). What does the play encourage us to feel about this belief?

12 Try performing Scene Seven in different ways to make Robbie's final description of his revelation about the world (*a*) ludicrous, (*b*) beautiful, (*c*) angry. What effects do the different versions have on our view of the play?

13 Discuss the significance of the many different images of fatherhood in this play.

14 Does this play offer any images of purity, goodness or utopia?

15 Elizabeth Young writes of Dennis Cooper that 'his central concern is something that has obsessed postmodern theorists. Faced with a seamlessly hyperreal society, apparently invulnerable to negation, criticism or political change, theorists have struggled to articulate a "real" that escapes representation' (Elizabeth Young and Graham Caveney, *Shopping in Space: Essays on American 'Blank Generation' Fiction*, London, Serpent's Tail, 1992, p. 260). Consider *Shopping and Fucking* in the light of this statement.

16 Is *Shopping and Fucking* a moral play?

DAN REBELLATO is senior lecturer in drama and theatre at Royal Holloway University of London. He has published on Ravenhill, Sarah Kane, David Greig, Suspect Culture, Rattigan, Coward and Dario Fo. His book on British theatre in the 1950s, *1956 and All That*, is published by Routledge, and he is currently completing a book on contemporary British drama and globalisation. He is also an award-winning playwright and translator.

Methuen Drama Student Editions

Jean Anouilh *Antigone* • John Arden *Serjeant Musgrave's Dance*
Alan Ayckbourn *Confusions* • Aphra Behn *The Rover* • Edward Bond
Lear • *Saved* • Bertolt Brecht *The Caucasian Chalk Circle* • *Fear and
Misery in the Third Reich* • *The Good Person of Szechwan* • *Life of Galileo* •
Mother Courage and her Children • *The Resistible Rise of Arturo Ui* • *The
Threepenny Opera* • Anton Chekhov *The Cherry Orchard* • *The Seagull* •
Three Sisters • *Uncle Vanya* • Caryl Churchill *Serious Money* • *Top Girls*
• Shelagh Delaney *A Taste of Honey* • Euripides *Elektra* • *Medea*•
Dario Fo *Accidental Death of an Anarchist* • Michael Frayn *Copenhagen*
• John Galsworthy *Strife* • Nikolai Gogol *The Government Inspector* •
Robert Holman *Across Oka* • Henrik Ibsen *A Doll's House* • *Ghosts*•
Hedda Gabler • Charlotte Keatley *My Mother Said I Never Should* •
Bernard Kops *Dreams of Anne Frank* • Federico García Lorca *Blood
Wedding* • *Doña Rosita the Spinster* (bilingual edition) •*The House of
Bernarda Alba* • (bilingual edition) • *Yerma* (bilingual edition) • David
Mamet *Glengarry Glen Ross* • *Oleanna* • Patrick Marber *Closer* • John
Marston *Malcontent* • Martin McDonagh *The Lieutenant of Inishmore* •
Joe Orton *Loot* • Luigi Pirandello *Six Characters in Search of an Author*
• Mark Ravenhill *Shopping and F***ing* • Willy Russell *Blood Brothers*
• *Educating Rita* • Sophocles *Antigone* • *Oedipus the King* • Wole
Soyinka *Death and the King's Horseman* • Shelagh Stephenson *The
Memory of Water* • August Strindberg *Miss Julie* • J. M. Synge *The
Playboy of the Western World* • Theatre Workshop *Oh What a Lovely
War* Timberlake Wertenbaker *Our Country's Good* • Arnold Wesker
The Merchant • Oscar Wilde *The Importance of Being Earnest* •
Tennessee Williams *A Streetcar Named Desire* • *The Glass Menagerie*

Methuen Drama Contemporary Dramatists

include

John Arden (two volumes)
Arden & D'Arcy
Peter Barnes (three volumes)
Sebastian Barry
Dermot Bolger
Edward Bond (eight volumes)
Howard Brenton
  (two volumes)
Richard Cameron
Jim Cartwright
Caryl Churchill (two volumes)
Sarah Daniels (two volumes)
Nick Darke
David Edgar (three volumes)
David Eldridge
Ben Elton
Dario Fo (two volumes)
Michael Frayn (three volumes)
David Greig
John Godber (four volumes)
Paul Godfrey
John Guare
Lee Hall (two volumes)
Peter Handke
Jonathan Harvey
  (two volumes)
Declan Hughes
Terry Johnson (three volumes)
Sarah Kane
Barrie Keeffe
Bernard-Marie Koltès
  (two volumes)
Franz Xaver Kroetz
David Lan
Bryony Lavery
Deborah Levy
Doug Lucie

David Mamet (four volumes)
Martin McDonagh
Duncan McLean
Anthony Minghella
  (two volumes)
Tom Murphy (six volumes)
Phyllis Nagy
Anthony Neilsen (two volumes)
Philip Osment
Gary Owen
Louise Page
Stewart Parker (two volumes)
Joe Penhall (two volumes)
Stephen Poliakoff
  (three volumes)
David Rabe (two volumes)
Mark Ravenhill (two volumes)
Christina Reid
Philip Ridley
Willy Russell
Eric-Emmanuel Schmitt
Ntozake Shange
Sam Shepard (two volumes)
Wole Soyinka (two volumes)
Simon Stephens (two volumes)
Shelagh Stephenson
David Storey (three volumes)
Sue Townsend
Judy Upton
Michel Vinaver
  (two volumes)
Arnold Wesker (two volumes)
Michael Wilcox
Roy Williams (three volumes)
Snoo Wilson (two volumes)
David Wood (two volumes)
Victoria Wood

Methuen Drama World Classics
include

Jean Anouilh (two volumes)
Brendan Behan
Aphra Behn
Bertolt Brecht (eight volumes)
Büchner
Bulgakov
Calderón
Čapek
Anton Chekhov
Noël Coward (eight volumes)
Feydeau (two volumes)
Eduardo De Filippo
Max Frisch
John Galsworthy
Gogol
Gorky (two volumes)
Harley Granville Barker
  (two volumes)
Victor Hugo
Henrik Ibsen (six volumes)
Jarry

Lorca (three volumes)
Marivaux
Mustapha Matura
David Mercer (two volumes)
Arthur Miller (six volumes)
Molière
Musset
Peter Nichols (two volumes)
Joe Orton
A. W. Pinero
Luigi Pirandello
Terence Rattigan
  (two volumes)
W. Somerset Maugham
  (two volumes)
August Strindberg
  (three volumes)
J. M. Synge
Ramón del Valle-Inclán
Frank Wedekind
Oscar Wilde

Methuen Drama Modern Plays

include work by

Edward Albee
Jean Anouilh
John Arden
Margaretta D'Arcy
Peter Barnes
Sebastian Barry
Brendan Behan
Dermot Bolger
Edward Bond
Bertolt Brecht
Howard Brenton
Anthony Burgess
Simon Burke
Jim Cartwright
Caryl Churchill
Complicite
Noël Coward
Lucinda Coxon
Sarah Daniels
Nick Darke
Nick Dear
Shelagh Delaney
David Edgar
David Eldridge
Dario Fo
Michael Frayn
John Godber
Paul Godfrey
David Greig
John Guare
Peter Handke
David Harrower
Jonathan Harvey
Iain Heggie
Declan Hughes
Terry Johnson
Sarah Kane
Charlotte Keatley
Barrie Keeffe

Howard Korder
Robert Lepage
Doug Lucie
Martin McDonagh
John McGrath
Terrence McNally
David Mamet
Patrick Marber
Arthur Miller
Mtwa, Ngema & Simon
Tom Murphy
Phyllis Nagy
Peter Nichols
Sean O'Brien
Joseph O'Connor
Joe Orton
Louise Page
Joe Penhall
Luigi Pirandello
Stephen Poliakoff
Franca Rame
Mark Ravenhill
Philip Ridley
Reginald Rose
Willy Russell
Jean-Paul Sartre
Sam Shepard
Wole Soyinka
Simon Stephens
Shelagh Stephenson
Peter Straughan
C. P. Taylor
Theatre Workshop
Sue Townsend
Judy Upton
Timberlake Wertenbaker
Roy Williams
Snoo Wilson
Victoria Wood

For a complete catalogue of Methuen Drama titles
write to:

Methuen Drama
36 Soho Square
London
W1D 3QY

or you can visit our website at:

www.methuendrama.com